BATMAN
THE DARK KNIGHT
GOLDEN DAWN

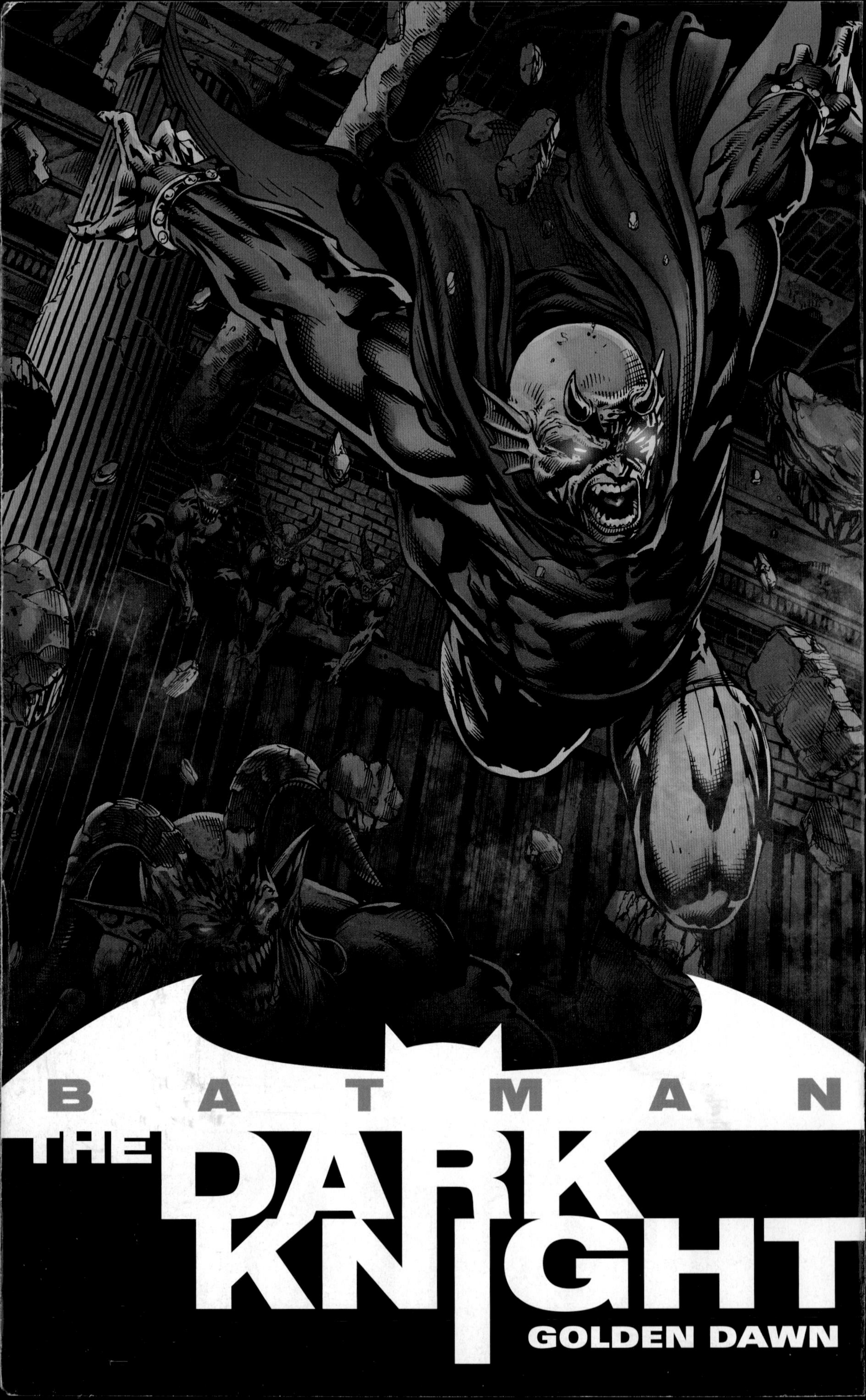
BATMAN
THE DARK KNIGHT
GOLDEN DAWN

DAVID FINCH Writer

DAVID FINCH JASON FABOK Pencillers

SCOTT WILLIAMS RICHARD FRIEND RYAN WINN BATT SAL REGLA JAIME MENDOZA RAY McCARTHY GREG ADAMS Inkers

DAVE SHARPE ROB LEIGH Letterers

ALEX SINCLAIR PETE PANTAZIS PETER STEIGERWALD TONY AVIÑA ALLEN PASSALAQUA Colorists

DAVID FINCH Cover Artist

Batman created by **BOB KANE**
The Demon created by **JACK KIRBY**

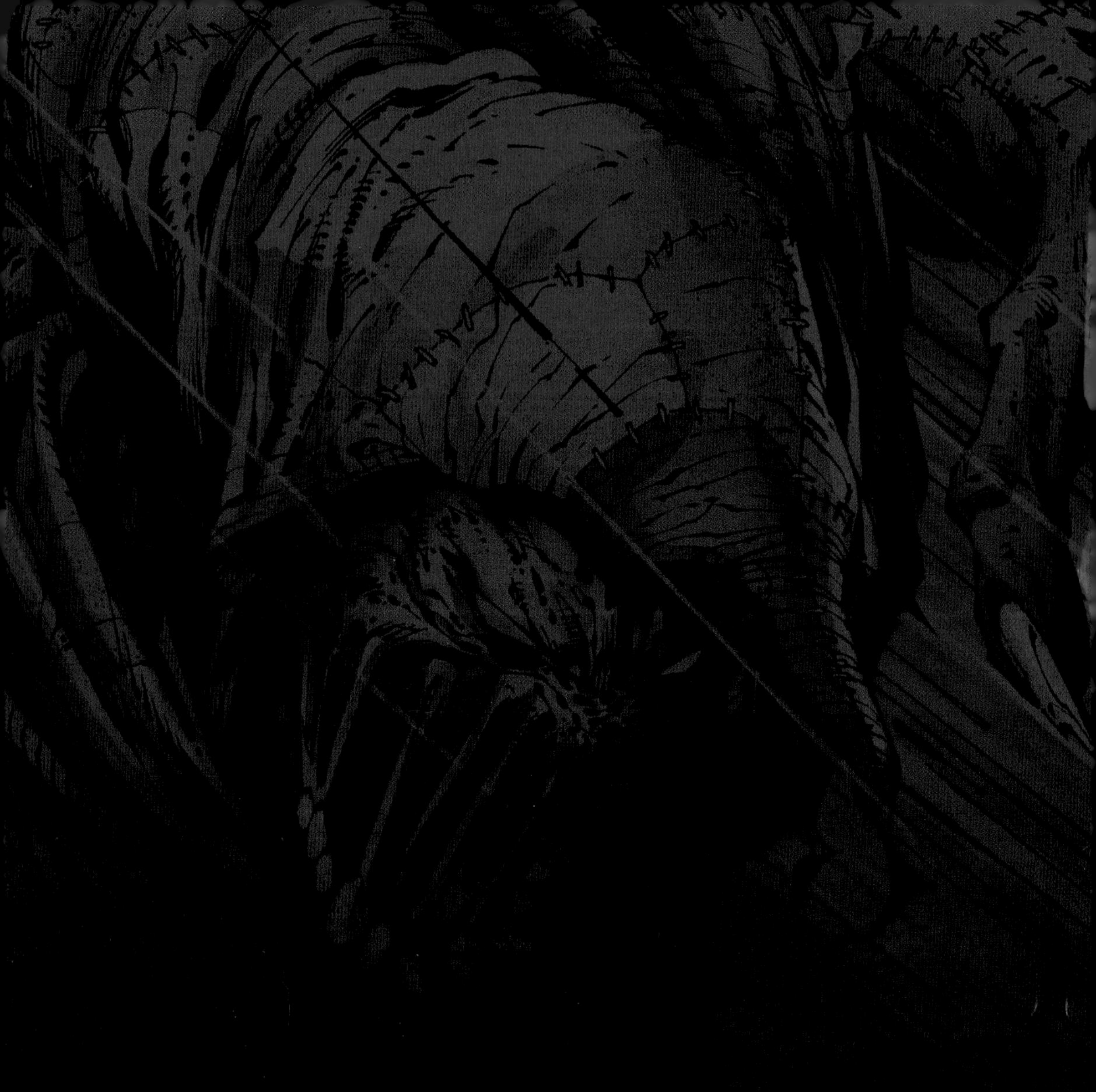

MIKE MARTS Editor – Original Series **JANELLE ASSELIN** Associate Editor – Original Series
KATIE KUBERT RICKEY PURDIN Assistant Editors – Original Series **PETER HAMBOUSSI** Editor
ROBBIN BROSTERMAN Design Director – Books **CURTIS KING JR.** Publication Design

BOB HARRAS VP – Editor-in-Chief

DIANE NELSON President **DAN DIDIO and JIM LEE** Co-Publishers **GEOFF JOHNS** Chief Creative Officer
JOHN ROOD Executive VP – Sales, Marketing and Business Development **AMY GENKINS** Senior VP – Business and Legal Affairs
NAIRI GARDINER Senior VP – Finance **JEFF BOISON** VP – Publishing Operations **MARK CHIARELLO** VP – Art Direction and Design
JOHN CUNNINGHAM VP – Marketing **TERRI CUNNINGHAM** VP – Talent Relations and Services **ALISON GILL** Senior VP – Manufacturing and Operations
HANK KANALZ Senior VP – Digital **JAY KOGAN** VP – Business and Legal Affairs, Publishing **JACK MAHAN** VP – Business Affairs, Talent
NICK NAPOLITANO VP – Manufacturing Administration **SUE POHJA** VP – Book Sales **COURTNEY SIMMONS** Senior VP – Publicity **BOB WAYNE** Senior VP – Sales

BATMAN – THE DARK KNIGHT: GOLDEN DAWN

DC Comics, 1700 Broadway, New York, NY 10019. A Warner Bros. Entertainment Company
Printed by RR Donnelley, Salem, VA, USA. 12/21/12. First Printing.
ISBN: 978-1-4012-3828-5

Library of Congress Cataloging-in-Publication Data

Finch, David, 1972-
Batman, the dark knight : golden dawn / David Finch, Jason Fabok.
p. cm.
"Originally published in single magazine form in Batman: The Dark Knight 1-5, Batman: The Return 1, Superman/Batman 75."
ISBN 978-1-4012-3828-5
1. Graphic novels. I. Fabok, Jay. II. Title. III. Title: Golden dawn.
PN6728.B36F56 2012
741.5'973—dc23

2012032146

Certified Chain of Custody
At Least 20% Certified Forest Content
www.sfiprogram.org
SFI-01042
APPLIES TO TEXT STOCK ONLY

BATMAN: THE DARK KNIGHT #1 cover
Art by **DAVID FINCH**

I haven't thought about her in years. I'd put her out of my mind after she broke my heart in college.
Now she's become an obsession.
I find myself searching my memory for her... all the way down to the dimly remembered days before my life was shattered forever.
Before I became what I am.
DAWN IS OUR GUEST, BRUCE. TRY TO BE A GOOD HOST.
BUT SHE WON'T DO ANYTHING! SHE HATES ME!
GIVE HER A CHANCE TO GET TO KNOW YOU.
I'M SORRY, ALEISTER. YOU WERE SAYING...?
THOMAS, PLEASE...NO NEED TO APOLOGIZE.
I remember that I hated her when we first met. She was sullen and aloof.
WHOOOSSH!!
It was as if she lived under a dark cloud.
BRUCE, WHY DON'T YOU AND DAWN RUN OUT AND GET SOME AIR. TRY TO HAVE SOME FUN.
I DON'T KNOW...
THEY'LL BE

My parents went to Europe for two months that summer.
I didn't sleep for three days when they left, and I cried for a lot longer than that.
Alfred was a good babysitter though, and looking back, maybe that time made it easier the next year when I lost my parents forever.
When they came home they brought me a kite. It was beautiful, and huge, and I loved it.
When I flew it I knew my parents were thinking about me, even while they were gone.
HEY!
HEY!
WHY DID YOU DO THAT!? NOW IT'S GONE FOREVER!

IT'S JUST A KITE, SILLY!
GET BACK HERE!

IT WAS MINE, AND YOU--

HA HA HA!
UM...
DON'T--

I would spend a few long days after that trying to find my kite.
But the truth is, at that moment, it was the furthest thing from my mind...

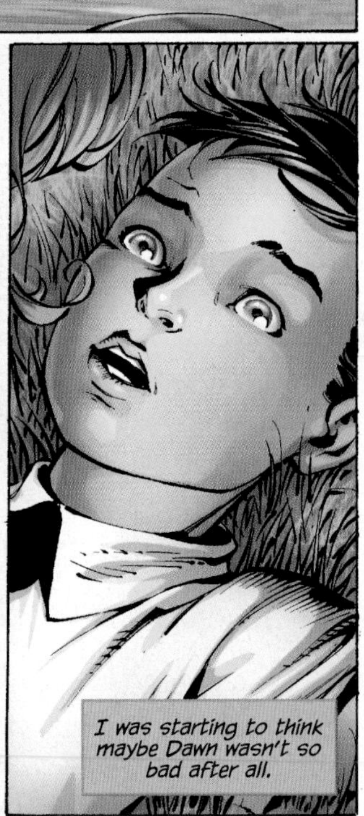
I was starting to think maybe Dawn wasn't so bad after all.

GOTHAM CITY.
NOW.
COMMISSIONER, I WASN'T TRANSFERRED FROM METROPOLIS TO HANDLE CARJACKINGS AND PURSE SNATCHING.
YOU *NEED* ME ON THE DAWN GOLDEN CASE.
THANKS, MACY.
SORRY, BOSS.
LOOK, FORBES, THE WORLD DOESN'T STOP WHEN A SOCIETY GIRL GOES MISSING. BAD THINGS STILL HAPPEN TO GOOD PEOPLE OUT THERE EVERY DAY.
YOU HAVE AN ASSIGNMENT, LIEUTENANT, AND THE PEOPLE OF GOTHAM NEED YOU ON IT.

BUT, COMMISSIONER--!
EXIT
WHAT D'YA GOT FOR ME, HARVEY?
A DAMN SANDWICH, BOSS.

PRESS IS CAMPED OUTSIDE.
WE GOT *JACK* FOR NEW LEADS.
AND MAYOR HADY HAS BEEN TRYING TO GET YOU ON THE HORN FOR THREE HOURS.
JAMES GORDON
COMMISSIONER
SIR, I HAVE THE MAYOR'S OFFICE ON LINE FOUR--
NOT NOW.

HAVE WE TRACKED DOWN EVERYONE WHO APPEARS ON MS. GOLDEN'S PHONE RECORDS?
JAMES GORDON
COMMISSIONER
YEAH. CAME UP EMPTY.
SEND A TEAM TO HER ADDRESS. DON'T WORRY ABOUT BEING NEAT THIS TIME. TEAR IT APART IF YOU HAVE TO.
FIND ME SOMETHING.

SLAMM
COMMISSIONER
HE ALWAYS LIKE THIS?
SHUT IT, NEW GUY.

It's cold and it's wet. The waiting is taking its toll.
I could go in and try to take him down now, but he's going to be dangerous enough outside where he'll be alone.
Innocent isn't the right word, but there are people... **uninvolved** inside.
SMASH
My patience pays off.
THANKS FOR GETTING THE DOOR FOR ME, ASS.
I feel a spike of adrenaline.
UGHNG
This won't be easy. Not that it ever is with **this one.**

I shadow him, wait for the right moment.
What is he--?
AHHHH...
HUH... WHA--?
MOVE ALONG, JERK! I'M TRYIN' TA GET SOME SLEEP HERE.
HURRRGGH!
OH, GOD...
OH, GOD...
OH, GOD...

Venom.
Croc is using it. Must be street grade...no way he got his hands on the pure formula.
This variation provides barely half the power with a few additional side effects.
His stagger tells me he's been strung out for days. But he'll still be strong. Stronger than he's ever been before.
Doesn't matter. I'm on a mission.
Find Dawn Golden or die trying.

BAR
I give him everything I've got--if this doesn't happen fast, it doesn't happen at all.
He barely feels it, but it's enough to knock him off balance. A good start.
WHAM!

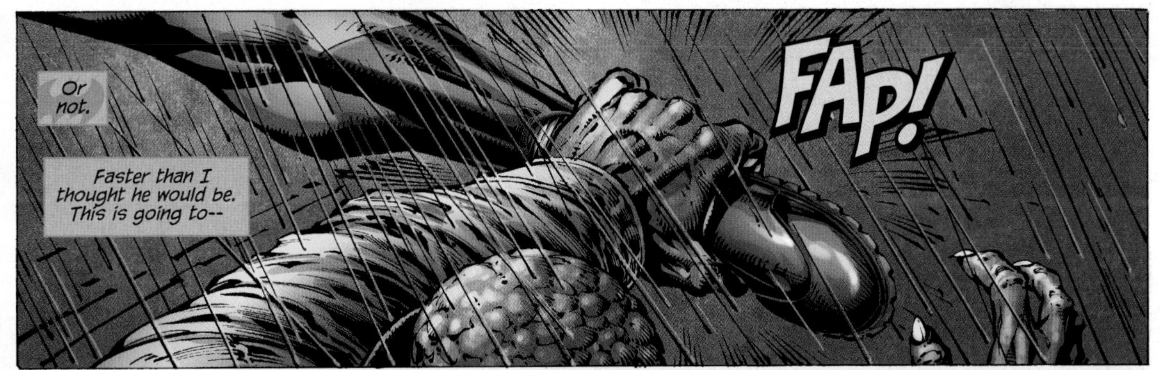
Or not.
Faster than I thought he would be. This is going to--
FAP!

CRRAASSSSHH!

RAAARRR!
His adrenaline is still spiking, he's not thinking straight. Need to use that.
SLAAMMMMMMMM!
ARRRGH!
Now is my chance. Time to fight dirty.

YOU THINK THIS IS GOING TO DO ANYTHING MORE THAN SLOW ME DOWN?
CALM DOWN, CROC. I NEED YOU TO ANSWER MY--
NGG!
Barely saw him move. I need to get a sample of this drug. I don't know enough--could get me killed.
URK--!
Need something to get him off me fast.
Blacking out. No. Can't.
GOOD NIGHT, BAT PUNK!
Need to improvise.
I hope this hurts.
WHA--?

SKRRASSSSHHHHH
I'm lucky to be standing. This was a stupid risk. Venom is on the streets, needed to be prepared for someone like Killer Croc getting their hands on it.
I WAS MINDIN' MY OWN BUSINESS. YOU ATTACKED ME.
YOU GOT NOTHING ON ME.
DAWN GOLDEN. RING ANY BELLS FOR YOU?
I DON'T KNOW WHAT YER TALKIN' ABOUT.
I need to stop trying to prove to myself that I'm back in the game, or I'll really be out for good.
WHAT'RE YOU...?
HEY! I GOT RIGHTS!

VENOM. THERE'S NO WAY TRASH LIKE YOU CAN AFFORD THE REAL DEAL. THIS STUFF IS MOSTLY POISON. BUT IT PACKS A PUNCH.
DAWN WENT MISSING LAST WEEK. YOU HEAR ANYTHING ABOUT THAT?
SERIOUSLY? YOU COME HERE ASKING FOR CURRENT EVENTS? DO I LOOK LIKE I WATCH THE NEWS?!
I BROUGHT SOMETHING FOR YOU, CROC.
IT IMMUNIZES THE BODY TO THE EFFECTS OF VENOM.
IT WORKS, BUT IT'S NOT PRETTY. YOU EVER GO OFF VENOM COLD TURKEY BEFORE? MOST PEOPLE DON'T SURVIVE IT.
DAWN. WHERE IS SHE? WHAT DID YOU DO WITH HER?
I...I DIDN'T KNOW WHO SHE WAS. I WAS OUT TAKING A WALK. JUST CLEARING MY HEAD. ALL OF A SUDDEN THIS GIRL IS IN FRONT OF ME.
WHERE WAS THIS?
FOURTH AND VICAR. DEVIL'S SQUARE.
I COULD TELL SHE WANTED IT. I JUST GAVE HER WHAT SHE WANTED!
AFTERWARDS SHE WAS PRETTY UPSET.
NO TELLING WITH CHICKS, RIGHT? A FRIEND OF MINE WANTED TO TAKE HER OUT AND SHOW HER A GOOD TIME. WHO AM I TO DENY A PAL? BESIDES, I DON'T THINK SHE LIKED ME FOR SOME REASON.
WHO DID YOU SELL HER TO? WHAT WAS HIS NAME?
SELL? WHOA... SLOW DOWN.
NAME!
L-LARS BECK.
DIRTBAG.
HEY, STOP! GURG... GUK!

HWAAAHH! PTHHHPPPT!

BAR
PAWN BROKERS
O'SULLIVA
HWAAAHH! ARRRGGHH! I'M GONNA KILL YOU, BATFREAK!
He just drank soda water and some food coloring.
STOP
I wish they were all so *easy.*
WE'VE GOT A MATCH ON YOUR GUY. LARS BECK. ALSO GOES BY LARS BECKER AND LARRY BOOKER. HE'S GOT A SHEET I COULD WALLPAPER MY OFFICE WITH.
NONE OF IT REALLY SERIOUS. SMALL-TIME STUFF. HE WAS WORKING OUT OF A NEW CLUB IN DEVIL'S SQUARE CALLED THE BOOM ROOM.
WAS?
HE WAS FISHED OUT OF THE GOTHAM RIVER THIS MORNING. HE WAS TIED DOWN, BUT IT DOESN'T LOOK LIKE THEY DID A VERY GOOD JOB.
HEY, THIS WAS GOOD WORK HERE TONIGHT. I HAVE TO THANK--
AR
COMMISSIONER! CAN I HAVE A WORD WITH YOU?
DOES THIS HAVE ANY CONNECTION TO THE DISAPPEARANCE OF DAWN GOLDEN? ARE YOU ANY CLOSER TO FINDING HER, OR WHAT MIGHT HAVE HAPPENED TO HER? AT WHAT POINT DOES THIS CEASE BEING A MISSING PERSONS CASE AND BECOME A MURDER CASE?
NO COMMENT.
INE DO NOT CROSS
COMMISSIONER! THE CITIZENS OF GOTHAM HAVE A RIGHT TO SOME *ANSWERS!*
LOOK, NO COMMENT. I'LL GIVE YOU ALL A BRIEFING TOMORROW.

THE NARROWS...
MAYBE REN OWED MONEY TO THE VIC AND HE SKIPPED TOWN.
NO WAY, MAN. NO WAY. THE VIC WON'T TAKE HIS ACTION NO MORE.
SOMEONE ELSE, THEN. REN ALWAYS BE INTO SOMEONE.
LAUND
ADULT
WHAT ABOUT JACKIE? ANYBODY SEEN HIM AROUND? OR MALLARD? NOBODY SEEN HIM FER WEEKS NOW.
FIRST MALLARD, THEN JACKIE, AND NOW REN. SOMETHIN'S GOIN' DOWN. I CAN *FEEL* IT.
YER ALL A BUNCHA OLD WOMEN. GOT NUTHIN' BETTER TA DO THAN STIR THE POT.
I'LL LEAVE YOU LADIES TO IT. GOTTA TAKE A LEAK.
YEAH? WADDA *YOU* KNOW, KING? I GOT A *SENSE* FOR THIS KINDA STUFF-- THIS AIN'T *RIGHT.*
SOMETHIN'S *OUT THERE,* MAN. SOMETHIN' *EVIL.* THEM GUYS *AIN'T* COMIN' BACK.
DUDE, IF YOU HAD A SENSE FOR STUFF YOU'DA KEPT PEOPLE HERE 'STEAD OF NOTICING WHEN THEY'RE GONE.
WHATEVER. WIPE THAT FREAKIN' BOTTLE OFF BEFORE YOU HAND IT BACK, BOURBON. I DON'T WANNA CATCH WHATEVER YOU G--
AAAAUUGGGHHGH!

KING!
NO! DON'T GO OUT THERE!
GET OFF ME!
KING!
OOOOH, MAN. KING, WHAT THE HELL--?!
L-LOOK AT HIS EYES! OH MY GOD, HE... OH, GOD...
HUAAARK!
ELECTRONICS

THE BATCAVE.
I HAVE MATTERS THAT ARE **FAR** MORE PRESSING THAN A SYSTEMS ANALYSIS ON YOUR NEW TOY, YOU SHOULD KNOW. AND IT WOULD CERTAINLY HELP IF EACH PART WAS NOT CODED IN A DIFFERENT LANGUAGE.
YOUR NEW FLAIR FOR GLOBALIZATION CERTAINLY COMES WITH ITS SHARE OF ANNOYANCES.
JOKER

MASTER BRUCE, I THINK THAT YOU FORGET THAT I AM **ALWAYS** HERE. MS. GOLDEN'S FACE HAS BEEN ON THAT SCREEN FOR DAYS NOW.
...NO. YEARS AGO. WHEN WE WERE SMALL CHILDREN.
I REMEMBER THAT SHE WAS A SULLEN CHILD. HER FATHER, ALEISTER... I NEVER CARED FOR HIM. SHE WAS A PRODUCT OF SUSPECT UPBRINGING.
YES.

SHE COULD NOT BE SAVED FROM HER FATHER THEN, AND SAVING HER NOW CANNOT CHANGE THAT, MASTER BRUCE. YOU DO UNDERSTAND THAT, I HOPE.
YOUR OBSESSION WITH THIS CASE IS BECOMING SLIGHTLY UNHEALTHY...

SPEAKING OF WHICH, YOU HAVE MORE PRESSING MATTERS AROUND THE WORLD VYING FOR YOUR ATTENTION AS WELL. JAPAN? ARGENTINA, PERHAPS?
AND YOUNG MASTER GRAYSON HAS PROVEN MORE THAN CAPABLE OF HANDLING GOTHAM CITY IN YOUR ABSENCE.
DO YOU REMEMBER DAWN GOLDEN, ALFRED?

LARS BECK. IF HE IS CONNECTED, I'M NOT SEEING IT HERE. EVERYTHING I CAN FIND JUST POINTS TO A SMALL-TIME CLUB OWNER WHO DEALT A LITTLE ON THE SIDE.
I CAN'T SHAKE THE FEELING THAT THERE'S A LOT MORE GOING ON HERE THAN MEETS THE EYE. I'M GOING UNDERCOVER TO ASK SOME QUESTIONS, BUT FIRST I WANT TO GET A GOOD LOOK AT THE PLACE WHILE IT'S CLOSED.
MAYBE SOMETHING WILL TURN UP.
ACCESS THE LOCAL GRID AND CUT THE POWER FOR A TWO-BLOCK RADIUS AROUND THE CLUB.
HAVE THE BATMOBILE READY TO GO IN TEN MINUTES.
YES, MASTER BRUCE.
I'M SO GLAD THAT WE HAD THIS CHANCE TO TALK...

The Boom Room. A seedy little meat market in the poor end of town. It's empty, but I don't expect to find Dawn waiting for me when I come in the back door.
Hopefully I can find something that brings me closer to finding her.
286

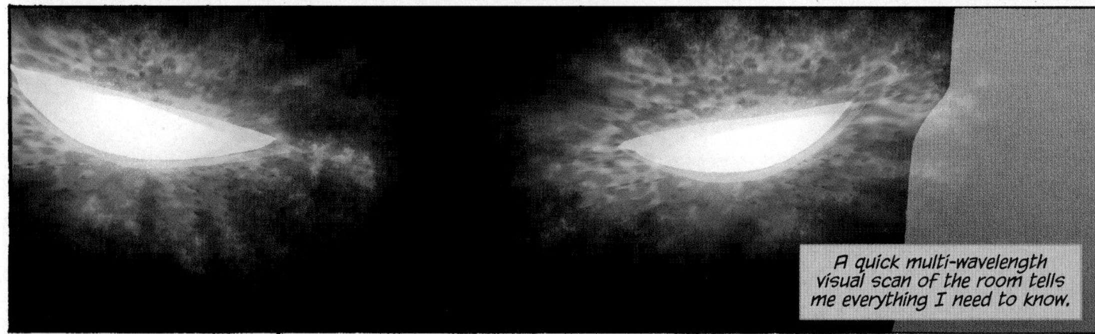
A quick multi-wavelength visual scan of the room tells me everything I need to know.

No need to kick over furniture.

ALFRED, ARE YOU SEEING THIS?

YES. IT SEEMS TO BE AN EXACT MATCH TO PHOTOS OF A NECKLACE THAT BELONGS TO DAWN GOLDEN.

I remember, as far back as our time together as children, her wearing this necklace. It's been wiped of any prints.
"I'LL HAVE TO GET IT BACK TO THE CAVE FOR FURTHER ANALYSIS, ALFRED."

"BUT SIR, WHY WOULD SOMEONE WIPE IT OF PRINTS BEFORE PUTTING IT IN THEIR OWN SAFE?"
"BECAUSE IT'S A *TRAP.*"

"THEN I SUGGEST YOU GET OUT OF THERE."
JACKPOT! TRACKER WORKED...
BEEP! ACCESS GRANTED.

C'MON... C'MON...
...SUCCESS!
SECURITY SYSTEMS DISABLED.

SIR, I'VE LOST THE CAR! IT'S BEEN TAKEN OFFLINE!

THAT'S IMPOSSIBLE! NO ONE COULD--
OH, EXCUSE ME. AM I *INTERRUPTING* SOMETHING?

I'M SOMETHING OF A NIGHT OWL LATELY, I SIMPLY CANNOT SLEEP. TOO MANY THINGS THAT REQUIRE MY EAGLE EYE.
AND WHO SHOULD I FIND STEALING EGGS FROM MY NEST?
BATMAN.
THESE MEN CARRY THE MOST ADVANCED MILITARY HARDWARE IN THE WORLD. YOU SIMPLY NEVER KNOW WHAT SORT OF RODENT MAY TURN UP.
THEY CANNOT MISS.
PENGUIN...

IN OTHER WORDS, YOUR GOOSE IS COOKED.

BATMAN: THE DARK KNIGHT #2 cover
Art by **DAVID FINCH, SCOTT WILLIAMS** and **PETER STEIGERWALD**

PENGUIN... WHAT HAVE YOU DONE WITH DAWN GOLDEN?!
PERHAPS YOU'VE NOTICED THAT I HAVE THE GUNS, BATMAN.
SO I'LL ASK THE QUESTIONS, IF YOU DON'T MIND.
DO YOU KNOW WHO DAWN IS? REALLY IS? ARE YOU SURE YOU WANT TO FIND OUT?
YOU SHOULD LEAVE WELL ENOUGH ALONE. SOME PEOPLE SIMPLY AREN'T WORTH IT.
IF YOU'VE HURT HER...

YOU HAVE MORE IMMEDIATE PAIN TO CONCERN YOURSELF WITH.
FIRE!
BRAKKA BRAKKA BRAKKA
YOU MISSED! THAT CAN'T HAPPEN WITH THESE GUNS!
WE'RE BEING JAMMED! I'VE GOT VISUAL ONLY.
NO... NO! JUST SHOOT!
BRAKKA BRAKKA BRAKKA
BRAKKA BRAKKA BRAKKA
PAF!

WHAT THE--?
I-IS IT OVER?
SOME KIND OF WIRE...
NO! YOU *IDIOT!*

ARG!
UHN!
ERK!
NO! NO! NO!
NO MORE GUNS. NOW I ASK THE QUESTIONS.

HWAAAAK!

HUFF HUFF

ARRRGGHH!
ZARRRK

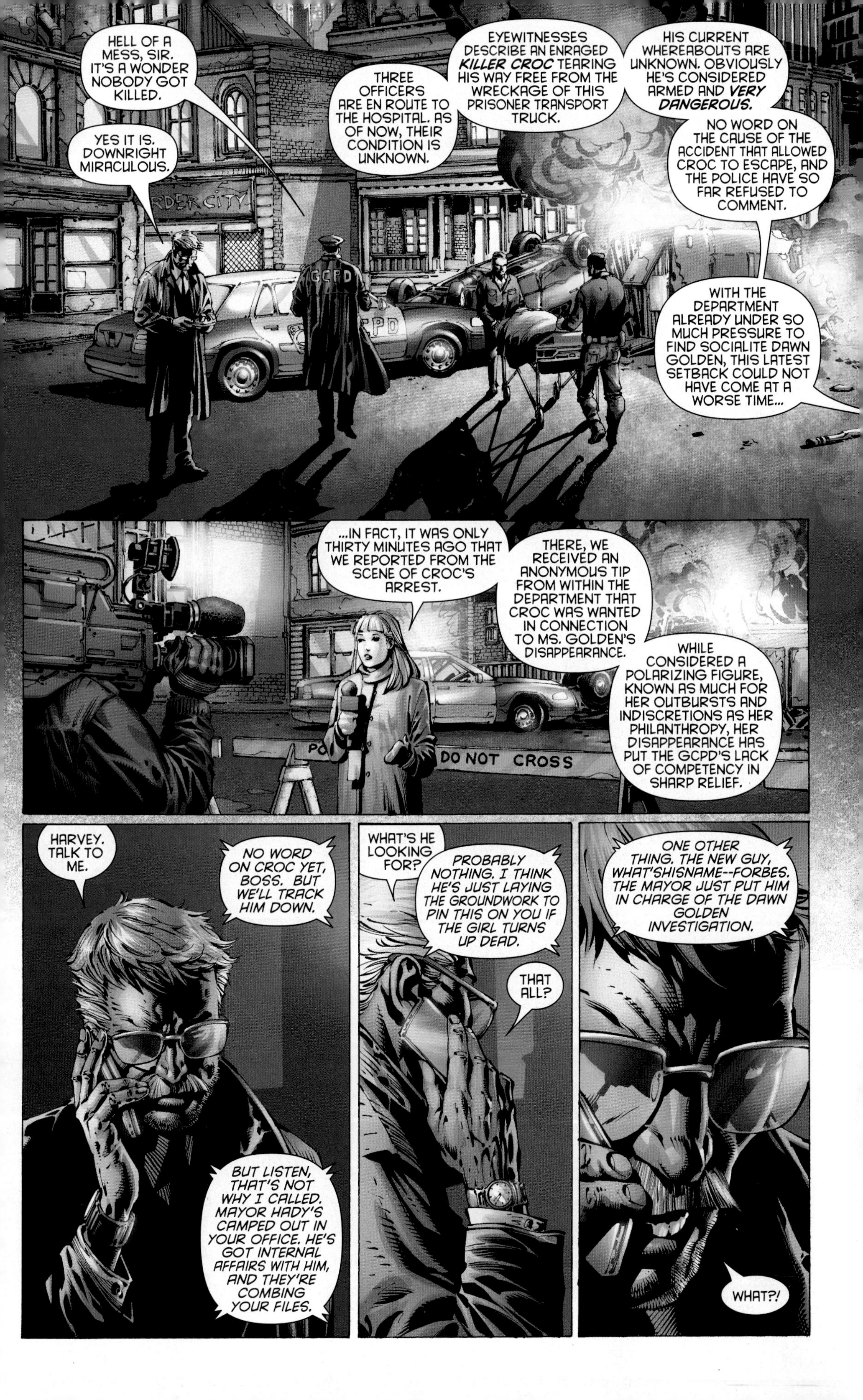
HELL OF A MESS, SIR. IT'S A WONDER NOBODY GOT KILLED.
YES IT IS. DOWNRIGHT MIRACULOUS.
THREE OFFICERS ARE EN ROUTE TO THE HOSPITAL. AS OF NOW, THEIR CONDITION IS UNKNOWN.
EYEWITNESSES DESCRIBE AN ENRAGED KILLER CROC TEARING HIS WAY FREE FROM THE WRECKAGE OF THIS PRISONER TRANSPORT TRUCK.
HIS CURRENT WHEREABOUTS ARE UNKNOWN. OBVIOUSLY HE'S CONSIDERED ARMED AND VERY DANGEROUS.
NO WORD ON THE CAUSE OF THE ACCIDENT THAT ALLOWED CROC TO ESCAPE, AND THE POLICE HAVE SO FAR REFUSED TO COMMENT.
WITH THE DEPARTMENT ALREADY UNDER SO MUCH PRESSURE TO FIND SOCIALITE DAWN GOLDEN, THIS LATEST SETBACK COULD NOT HAVE COME AT A WORSE TIME...
GCPD
...IN FACT, IT WAS ONLY THIRTY MINUTES AGO THAT WE REPORTED FROM THE SCENE OF CROC'S ARREST.
THERE, WE RECEIVED AN ANONYMOUS TIP FROM WITHIN THE DEPARTMENT THAT CROC WAS WANTED IN CONNECTION TO MS. GOLDEN'S DISAPPEARANCE.
WHILE CONSIDERED A POLARIZING FIGURE, KNOWN AS MUCH FOR HER OUTBURSTS AND INDISCRETIONS AS HER PHILANTHROPY, HER DISAPPEARANCE HAS PUT THE GCPD'S LACK OF COMPETENCY IN SHARP RELIEF.
DO NOT CROSS
HARVEY. TALK TO ME.
NO WORD ON CROC YET, BOSS. BUT WE'LL TRACK HIM DOWN.
BUT LISTEN, THAT'S NOT WHY I CALLED. MAYOR HADY'S CAMPED OUT IN YOUR OFFICE. HE'S GOT INTERNAL AFFAIRS WITH HIM, AND THEY'RE COMBING YOUR FILES.
WHAT'S HE LOOKING FOR?
PROBABLY NOTHING. I THINK HE'S JUST LAYING THE GROUNDWORK TO PIN THIS ON YOU IF THE GIRL TURNS UP DEAD.
THAT ALL?
ONE OTHER THING. THE NEW GUY, WHAT'SHISNAME--FORBES. THE MAYOR JUST PUT HIM IN CHARGE OF THE DAWN GOLDEN INVESTIGATION.
WHAT?!

LIVE SAT. OCT
IN CONCERT
HUFF! HUFF!
HUFF!
WAAHHH!
THWIPP!
DAWN GOLDEN. WHERE IS SHE?
THIS IS A *PRIVATE ESTABLISHMENT!* YOU CAN'T JUST BREAK IN AND GO THROUGH PEOPLE'S THINGS!
I'LL HAVE YOU BROUGHT UP ON CHARGES!

I'M NOT PLAYING GAMES, PENGUIN!
IF ANYTHING HAS HAPPENED TO HER...
W-WHY DO YOU CARE? WHAT IS SHE TO YOU, ANYWAY?
CRACK!
ARRGGHH!
WHERE IS SHE?! TALK!
GAHH!
CRACK!
WAAHH! STOP! PLEASE, STOP!
WRONG ANSWER.
CRACK!
SIR...WHAT ARE YOU DOING?
TALK!

ENOUGH.
WAAAHH! GET HIM OFF!
CHUDDD
I THOUGHT HE WAS ONE OF THE GOOD GUYS!
WAAAHHH...
SLAM!
SEE HOW YOU LIKE IT, BATFREAK.
BOSS, YOU OKAY?
WHERE WERE YOU?! LOOK WHAT HE DID TO ME!

MEANWHILE, OUTSIDE...
SUCCESS!
SECURITY SYSTEMS DISABLED.

CAN'T BELIEVE IT ACTUALLY WORKED!

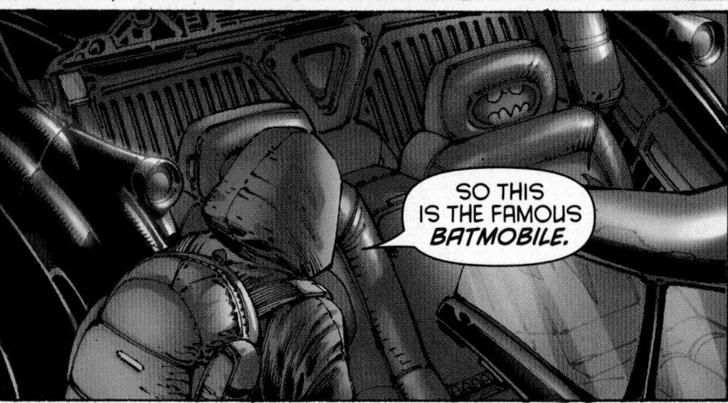
SO THIS IS THE FAMOUS *BATMOBILE.*

OW! BE CAREFUL, YOU SCALY BRUTE!
YOU WEIGH A LOT FOR SUCH A LITTLE GUY.

WATCH YOUR MOUTH, INGRATE! I'LL HAVE YOU KNOW, I EAT LIKE A *BIRD!*
I SHOULD HAVE YOU STRUNG UP BY YOUR TOES FOR LEAVING ME TO THAT SAVAGE!

CLOSE CANOPY!
SHOOK

DRIVE!
C'MON... C'MON.
IGNITION!
ALL RIGHT!
VROOMMM!

YOUR GUY TOOK HIS SWEET TIME TO BREAK ME OUT, BOSS.
I GOT HERE FAST AS I COULD.
AAAHHHH!
CRASSSH!

WHOA! STOP! STOPPP!

WAS THAT THE BATMOBILE I JUST SAW DRIVE AWAY?
JUST GET US OUT OF HERE, YOU LUMMOX.

THE NARROWS.
I CAN'T GET KING OUTTA MY HEAD...HOW HE DIED...
...WHAT COULDA DONE THAT TO HIM?
WHATEVER IT WAS, IT'S TAKING US OUT ONE BY ONE.
I'M NOT HANGING AROUND TO FIND OUT WHO'S NEXT.
ROGUES
GALLERY
YEAH? WHERE YOU GONNA GO? THIS PLACE IS ALL WE KNOW.
I GOT IDEAS. ANYWAY, IT'S GOTTA BE BETTER THAN HERE.
YOU CAN'T JUST CUT OUT ON US, MANNY. WE'VE ALWAYS STUCK TOGETHER.
WE JUST GOTTA KEEP EACH OTHER CLOSE. NOBODY EVER GOT HIT WHEN THEY WASN'T ALONE.
NO. I CAN FEEL THAT THING OUT THERE. IT'S *WATCHIN'* US, ALL THE TIME.
IF WE STAY HERE, WE'LL WIND UP JUST LIKE KING BEFORE WE KNOW WHAT HIT US.
WE'RE THE ONLY FAMILY YOU GOT. ***DON'T*** FORGET THAT.
YOU LET SOME MONSTER CHASE YOU AWAY, YOU'LL BE LEFT WITH NOTHIN'. YOU'RE BETTER OFF DYIN' HERE.

HE'S RIGHT, MANNY. WE GOT NUTHIN' BUT EACH OTHER. THERE'S NOWHERE FOR US TO GO.
I-I GOT FAMILY OUT THERE...BUT THEY STOPPED CALLING ME THAT A LONG TIME AGO.
ANYWAY, WHAT MONSTER WANTS TO BE OUT IN *THIS?*
KRAKOOOOOM!
HAHA. THAT'S THE SPIRIT, BUDDY. I'M SURE WE'RE FINE TONIGHT.

THE RESIDENCE OF JASON BLOOD.
TOO MANY SIGNS TO IGNORE.
SIGH
I CAN'T SIT THIS ONE OUT. LIKE IT OR NOT, NEITHER OF US CAN.
CHANGE! CHANGE, O FORM OF MAN.
RELEASE THE MIGHT FROM FLESHY MIRE.
BOIL THE BLOOD IN HEART OF FIRE!
GONE! GONE, THE FORM OF MAN...
RISE, THE DEMON...

ETRIGAN!

UGN...
Rusty blades are twisting in my head. Hard to focus through the pain.
Where am I?
I-I remember. The bar.
Finding Dawn's necklace. Holding it in my hand.
Then rage. Too strong to fight... I didn't want to fight.
What have I done?!
The amulet! Where is it?
It's gone. I can feel it. And the rage is gone with it.

Have to get ou--
SLAMMMM!
LOOK WHO'S AWAKE.

JUST IN TIME FOR THE MORNING SHOW.
YOU'LL HAVE TO EXCUSE THE IMPERSONAL NATURE OF THIS EXCHANGE, BATMAN.
I'M SLIGHTLY INCAPACITATED AT THE MOMENT. AND SINCE I HAVE YOU TO THANK FOR MY CURRENT STATE, I'VE TAKEN THE LIBERTY OF ARRANGING A SMALL TOKEN OF MY APPRECIATION.

WATCH!
LET ME SWITCH TO A MORE INTERESTING SCENE THAN MY SMILING FACE.
DAWN GOLDEN. I THINK THE LIGHTING CAPTURES HER WELL.
NO!

BUT I'M NOT SURE HOW LONG SHE CAN SURVIVE THE HEAT.
YOU MANIAC!

OH, I THINK WE BOTH KNOW WHO THE REAL MANIAC IS NOW.
ENJOY THE SHOW!

TRY NOT TO GET TOO EXCITED. THOSE BOMBS ARE SET TO YOUR HEART RATE!
WAHA HAHAH!

GOTHAM CITY... THE NARROWS.
HUFF HUFF WHEEZE
HUFF HUFF

N-NO!
ROAARRR!
AAAHHHHHH!

BATMAN: THE DARK KNIGHT #3 cover
Art by **DAVID FINCH, SCOTT WILLIAMS** and **ALEX SINCLAIR**

RRRRRGGGGHHHH!
AAAAAAHHHHHHHH!

W-WHAT *ARE* YOU?! GET OFF ME!

N-NO, *PLEASE!*
YOUR FUN HAS COME TO AN *END,* LITTLE DEMON...

SPLOORRCH!
RARRRGGGH!

THE BALANCE MUST BE MAINTAINED!
SSLAAASSSSSSHH!
I KNOW WHO YOU ARE...WHERE IS YOUR RHYME, DEMON?
YOUR POWER IS GONE. YOU CANNOT STOP ME!
HAHA! THEN IT IS TRUE. YOU HAVE LOST YOUR STATUS!
RRAARRGGHH!
YOU SHOULD NOT HAVE COME. THERE WILL BE A PRICE!
TH-THANKS!
I THOUGHT I WAS A GONER FOR SURE!
I DID NOT COME TO SAVE YOU, HUMAN.

AAHHHHH!
MAKE IT STOP!
OH NO! OH NO!
WHO IS THIS?! WHAT DO YOU THINK YOU'RE DOING?
TRYING NOT TO GET KILLED! HOW DO YOU DRIVE THIS THING?!
YOU DON'T! BUT SEEING AS YOU ARE, PERHAPS I SHOULD HELP BEFORE SOMEONE GETS HURT.
THANKS!
HEY, WHO ARE YOU, ANYWAY?

LIQU
Restaurant
I'M YOUR FRIEND. YOU KNOW THAT, RIGHT?
I KNOW THAT, HARVEY. I DO. BUT I'VE GOT IT UNDER CONTROL.
FORBES ISN'T JUST GUNNING FOR YOUR JOB, BOSS. IT'S BIGGER THAN THAT.
FORBES IS JUST TOO AMBITIOUS FOR HIS OWN GOOD. IT'S GONNA GET HIM IN TROUBLE SOON ENOUGH.
YOU'VE BEEN AROUND THE BLOCK, BULLOCK, SO YOU SHOULD KNOW HOW THIS GAME PLAYS OUT.
NOT THIS TIME, JIM. THE DAWN GOLDEN THING IS KILLING US IN THE PRESS.
AND CROC'S ESCAPE COULDN'T HAVE COME AT A WORSE TIME.
IT WAS AN INSIDE JOB, AND I THINK FORBES WAS INVOLVED. HE WAS IN--
YOU EVER THINK THAT MAYBE IT'S JUST MY TIME? NOBODY STAYS AT THE TOP JOB FOREVER.
TELL YOU THE TRUTH, I'M TIRED, BUDDY.
FORBES WANTS IT SO BAD, HE CAN HAVE IT.
AW, I APPRECIATE THE SENTIMENT.
BUT I'M JUST HERE TO DO WHAT I CAN FOR THE GOOD PEOPLE OF THIS FINE CITY.
HEY, I'M NOT INTERRUPTING, AM I?

I HOPE YOU DON'T MIND MY SAYING, COMMISSIONER, BUT YOU DON'T LOOK GOOD. YOU SHOULD REALLY GET SOME REST.
MAYBE YOU SHOULD TAKE SOME TIME WITH THE FAMILY.
I THINK I HEAR YOUR MOTHER CALLING YOU IN FOR SUPPER, FORBES.
WE WERE HAVING AN ADULT CONVERSATION HERE.
YOU BETTER LEARN TO SHOW SOME PROPER RESPECT, OLD MAN.
GET OUTTA HERE BEFORE I GIVE YOU A SPANKING YOU WON'T FORGET.
YEAH? LET'S TAKE THIS OUTSIDE AND SEE WHAT YOU GOT!
YOU'RE HISTORY, OLD MAN! YOU'VE LOST IT! THE ONLY ONE WHO DOESN'T KNOW THAT IS YOU!
GET HIM OUT OF HERE!
WE GOT HIM, SIR.

MEANWHILE...
WATCH THE TV!
YOU GOT ME, PENGUIN...
...JUST LET DAWN GO.
SHE'S OF NO VALUE TO YOU NOW.

NOT TRUE! AFTER ALL, WHO CAN PUT A PRICE ON REVENGE?
THAT WRETCHED GIRL DESERVES EVERYTHING THAT'S COMING TO HER AND MORE.
LET ME TELL YOU A FUNNY STORY...
OF COURSE, I WAS THE ONLY ONE WHO WASN'T LAUGHING.

WE MET AT THE GOTHAM SOCIAL CLUB. SHE WAS SO VERY CHARMING AND BEAUTIFUL. I WAS IMMEDIATELY SMITTEN.
I LAVISHED HER WITH GIFTS AND OFFERED TO ESCORT HER TO THE WINTER BALL. IT WAS A BEAUTIFUL EVENT AT THE ICEBERG. YOU SHOULD REALLY TRY TO MAKE IT SOME...OH. WELL, I SUPPOSE NOT.
ON THE DAY OF THE BALL, I GAVE HER AN ENORMOUS DIAMOND, AND WE STRODE DOWN THE RED CARPET TOGETHER. I WAS POSITIVELY PREENING.

WHAT COULD THIS POSSIBLY HAVE TO DO WITH--
IT WAS A BEAUTIFUL MOMENT. A SOCIAL TRIUMPH!
AND THEN HER FRIENDS STARTED TO ARRIVE. EACH GIRL HAD WITH HER A MAN MORE GROTESQUE THAN THE LAST! WE WERE A FREAKSHOW! A GAG FOR THE CAMERAS!
I WAS HUMILIATED.

THAT KIND OF PAIN DOESN'T GO EASILY FORGOTTEN, BATMAN.
BUT I TIRE OF THIS GAME. YOUR BOMB WILL GO OFF IN...AH, EIGHT SECONDS NOW.
JUST THOUGHT YOU SHOULD KNOW.
WHAT?!

CRASSH!
WHEN WERE YOU GOING TO TELL ME THAT?!
I'M OUTTA HERE! YOU'RE ON YOUR OWN, BATMAN!
GONNA KILL THAT BACK-STABBIN' BIRD TURD!

NNNN!
NHARGH!

Dawn is nearby. I'm sure of it.
Croc is too lazy to find more than one place to hide out.
And I saw wires leading down these stairs.
Might as well have left me a trail of breadcrumbs.

JUST A LITTLE LIGHTER ON THE THROTTLE.
GOOD. I THINK YOU'VE GOT IT.
THANK YOU! I NEVER THOUGHT ABOUT HOW A VEHICLE LIKE THIS WOULD DRIVE. I JUST FIGURED IT WOULD BE LIKE ANY OTHER CAR, YOU KNOW?
THIS IS NOT JUST ANY CAR. BUT YOU KNEW THAT. I DIDN'T THINK IT WAS POSSIBLE FOR SOMEONE TO FIND A WAY TO OVERRIDE THE SECURITY SYSTEMS.
WHY DON'T YOU TELL ME WHY YOU'VE TAKEN THE BATMOBILE? YOU DON'T LOOK LIKE A CRIMINAL TO ME. BUT I SUPPOSE I HAVE BEEN WRONG BEFORE...
WAIT, YOU CAN SEE ME?!
OF COURSE I CAN. YOU DON'T SEEM TO KNOW VERY MUCH ABOUT WHAT YOU'VE STOLEN.
GREAT. JUST GREAT.
PLEASE, YOU MUST NOT DO THIS.
WHOEVER--OR WHATEVER--IS FORCING YOU TO DO THIS WON'T JUST WALK AWAY WHEN THEY GET THE CAR.
I-I'M ONLY DOING WHAT I HAVE TO DO. YOU DON'T UNDERSTAND!
I UNDERSTAND MORE THAN YOU MIGHT THINK.
THEY WON'T LET YOU LIVE, I PROMISE YOU!
...OKAY. JUST TELL ME WHERE I NEED TO TAKE IT. I JUST WANT TO GET OUT.

Her chest is still moving. She's alive, but barely.
The heat in here is **unbearable.**

Every second counts.
She's so beautiful, it takes my breath away. I have to force myself not to stare.
DAWN, I NEED TO GET YOU OUT OF HERE. DO YOU UNDERSTAND?

UHNNNN...

SO HOT...
COUGH-COUGH
I NEED WATER.

LET'S GET YOU OUT OF THIS ROOM FIRST.
BATMAN?
DON'T WORRY ABOUT THAT RIGHT NOW. CAN YOU STAND?
I-I DON'T KNOW.
I'LL CARRY YOU.

The Batmobile? Odd...
...but a lifesaver, nonetheless.
Who?

Dawn may be in shock.

She doesn't say anything. I don't force the issue.

HUFF HUFF

HOW COULD I BE SO STUPID?!

AND NOW WHAT AM I GOING TO DO?

OUR LITTLE BIRD HAS FLOWN THE COOP, IT WOULD SEEM. AND BATMAN IS WITH HER.
DO YOU HAVE ANY BRIGHT IDEAS BEFORE THE POLICE KICK IN THE DOOR?
I DID EVERYTHING YOU ASKED, JUST THE WAY YOU ASKED FOR IT TO BE DONE!
NOW IT'S TIME FOR YOU TO LIVE UP TO YOUR END OF THE BARGAIN!
I THINK THAT YOU DID WONDERFULLY! BUT I DIDN'T COME HERE TO TELL YOU THAT.
I NEED YOU TO DO ONE MORE THING FOR ME, I'M AFRAID.

JUST ONE MORE VERY SMALL THING.
I NEED YOU TO OPEN THE GATES OF HELL!

BATMAN: THE DARK KNIGHT #4 cover
Art by **DAVID FINCH, SCOTT WILLIAMS** and **ALEX SINCLAIR**

GOTHAM CITY. DEVIL'S SQUARE.
YOU KNEW THE TERMS WHEN YOU ACCEPTED OUR MONEY.
YOU MUST DELIVER...OR FACE THE CONSEQUENCES.
B-B-BUT YOU HAVE TO UNDERSTAND--
WE UNDERSTAND PERFECTLY WELL.
YOU HAVE ONE WEEK. AFTER THAT...
...YOUR FAMILY WILL SETTLE YOUR DEBT...

...IN BLOOD!
NO! YOU CAN'T--!
YOU HAVE A WEEK.
BUT I'VE BEEN FIRED! I NO LONGER HAVE ACCESS TO WAYNE INDUSTRIES' SECRETS! I'VE BEEN TRYING TO TELL YOU THA--
ENOUGH! NO MORE EXCUSES!
ONE WEEK!
PLEASE, OLD MAN-- DISAPPOINT ME. I HAVEN'T KILLED A WHOLE FAMILY FOR AT LEAST A YEAR.
I MISS THE PLEASURE.

SHOOK

WHERE...?
C'MON, C'MON.
NO! NO!
SHAKE SHAKE
I CAN'T HAVE LEFT IT IN THE BATMOBILE! PLEASE, NO.
NOO!
SMASH
MIRA? ARE YOU ALL RIGHT DOWN THERE?
YEAH... SORRY, DAD, I'M FINE. I JUST TRIPPED OVER MY CHAIR.
YOU SHOULD BE IN BED!
JUST FIVE MORE MINUTES, DAD!

MEANWHILE... IN THE SEWERS OF GOTHAM.
I KNOW YOU ARE CLOSE, LITTLE DEMON... I CAN SMELL YOUR FEAR.
SPLASH
COME OUT, COME OUT, LITTLE ONE...COME FACE ETRIGAN!

AARRGGHH!
TREACHEROUS FOOL! WE ARE FAR TOO POWERFUL FOR YOU NOW!
KA-SPLOOSH

Dawn hasn't spoken since I found her and ended the biggest manhunt Gotham has seen in recent memory.
O'BOYL
WENIGERS
GEORGE WENIGER'S FURNITURE
She might still be in shock.
SARAHS
The Penguin will pay for what he's done to her.
W-WHERE ARE WE GOING?
JUST TRY TO RELAX, DAWN. YOU'VE BEEN THROUGH A LOT, BUT YOU'RE SAFE NOW.
NO. YOU DON'T UNDERSTAND. I'M NOT SAFE. I CAN NEVER BE SAFE!
HE'LL FIND ME!
I'LL DEAL WITH PENGUIN. YOU DON'T NEED TO WORRY--
NO!
"NOT PENGUIN--I'VE BEEN RUNNING MUCH LONGER THAN THAT.
"SINCE I WAS A LITTLE GIRL, THE ONLY PLACE I EVER FELT REALLY SAFE WAS IN MY HEAD."

"I WAS HIS TROPHY FOR EVERY GALA AND EVENT IN GOTHAM.
"MY FATHER... MY FATHER KEPT ME AS HIS PRISONER.
"HE TOLD ME THAT MY SOUL BELONGED TO A GREATER CAUSE. HE HAD SO MANY FOLLOWERS, I THOUGHT HE MUST BE RIGHT.
"I SAT NUMBLY THROUGH DARK AND TWISTED RITUALS...WONDERING... WOULD I BE NEXT...?
"I WAS SCREAMING INSIDE, BUT THE SOUND WAS BECOMING A DISTANT ECHO."
BUT...YOUR FATHER IS DEAD. HE CAN'T HURT YOU NOW--
PLEASE. J-JUST LISTEN.
"THE RITUALS CONTINUED UNTIL EVENTUALLY MY FATHER'S BODY FAILED HIM. HE WAS DYING.
"AND I...I WAS GLAD. THE SMALL PART OF ME THAT COULD STILL FEEL ANYTHING GLIMMERED WITH HOPE THAT I COULD SOON BE FREE."

"HE LAY THERE WASTED AND DYING AND ALONE, BUT HE WOULDN'T LET ME GO SO EASILY.
"ON THE NIGHT THAT HE DIED, HE CALLED ME OVER TO HIS BEDSIDE--MY LEGS MOVED AGAINST MY WILL.
"HE REACHED OUT AND TOOK MY AMULET IN HIS HAND.
"IT WAS THE AMULET HE GAVE ME WHEN I WAS BORN. HE ALWAYS TOLD ME THAT IT MARKED ME FOR A HIGHER CALLING.
"I WAS TO BE SACRIFICED SO THAT HE COULD BECOME HELL'S LORD ON EARTH. IT WAS MY DUTY...MY PRIVILEGE...
"HE SCREAMED AND STRUCK OUT AT ME, BUT HE WAS TOO FRAIL. I DODGED HIM EASILY. IT WAS THE FIRST TIME I EVER DISOBEYED HIM.
"MY HEAD WAS SPINNING, BUT HIS HOLD ON ME BROKE. I RAN AND RAN AND NEVER LOOKED BACK."
DAWN, HE WAS AN EVIL, CRAZY MAN.
BUT HE'S DEAD NOW.
I THOUGHT SO, TOO.

GOTHAM CITY POLICE HEADQUARTERS.
GCPD
MACY!
MACY, WHERE'S LIEUTENANT FORBES? I NEED A WORD WITH HIM.
Um, HE'S IN YOUR OFFICE, SIR.
JAMES GORDON
COMMISSIONER
JUST WHAT THE BLAZES DO YOU THINK YOU'RE DOING, LIEUTENANT?
HAHA, YEAH, I HEAR YOU, BUDDY. HEY, IF YOU'RE NOT DOING ANYTHING THIS WEEKEND YOU SHOULD BRING THE KIDS BY FOR A SWIM IN THE POOL.
FORBES-- I'M TALKING TO YOU!

HANG ON JUST A SEC, BOBBY.
I'LL BE WITH YOU IN A MINUTE, JAMES. TAKE A SEAT.
GET THE HELL OFF MY PHONE! YOU'VE STEPPED WAY OVER THE LINE, LIEUTENANT!
WHOA, SLOW DOWN, OLD MAN. DON'T GIVE YOURSELF A HEART ATTACK.
AND YOU'RE BARGING INTO MY OFFICE NOW. STRAIGHT FROM MAYOR HADY.
YOU'RE ON PAID LEAVE. I BEGGED HIM TO LET ME TELL YOU MYSELF.
WHAT?! I'LL DRAG YOU OUTTA HERE MYSELF, YOU SMUG LITTLE PUNK!
TEMPER, TEMPER, JAMES. DON'T WANT TO ADD ASSAULT TO YOUR LIST OF CHARGES.
YOU'RE IN ENOUGH TROUBLE AS IT IS.
SLAM
STREET-GRADE VENOM. NASTY STUFF. YOU'VE BEEN UNDER INVESTIGATION FOR A LONG TIME ON THIS, JAMES.
SUCH A SHAME, TOO. I HATE TO SEE A COP DISGRACE HIMSELF AND THE FORCE LIKE THIS.
WHAT KIND OF AMATEUR HOUR GARBAGE IS THIS?! I'M GOING TO HAVE YOU STRIPPED DOWN TO PARKING ENFORCEMENT, YOU WEASEL!
AND ANOTHER THING...

"...I KNOW BATMAN IS IN ON IT, TOO."
WE'RE ALMOST TO YOUR APARTMENT.
YOU NEED TO MAKE YOURSELF PRESENTABLE BEFORE I TAKE YOU DOWN TO TALK TO COMMISSIONER GORDON.
YOU'RE GOING TO HAVE EVERY NEWS OUTLET IN GOTHAM AND BEYOND ON YOU THE MINUTE IT'S REVEALED YOU'VE BEEN FOUND.
WHAT?! NO! YOU CAN'T DO THAT!
PLEASE, HE'LL FIND ME AGAIN.
PLEASE BELIEVE ME. IF I'M ON THE NEWS, HE'LL FIND ME AND KILL ME! YOU HAVE TO PROTECT ME!

YOU ARE TOO WEAK TO STAND AGAINST US, ETRIGAN! YOU HAVE BEEN DISGRACED, AND YOUR POWER IS *GONE.* YOU HAVE EVEN LOST YOUR *RHYME!*
CRACK
I HAVE STRENGTH ENOUGH TO DEAL WITH THE LIKES OF *YOU,* LITTLE DEMON!
YOU STAND AGAINST FORCES THAT YOU CAN'T *POSSIBLY UNDERSTAND.* YIELD AND YOU MAY HAVE A ROLE IN HELL'S DOMINATION OF THIS PLANE!
FWIP
FWIP
WHAT FORCES? YOU ARE *ALONE!*
SSHRRIPP
AARRGH!
MAYBE THERE *IS* SOMEONE ELSE IN THERE WITH YOU, RAGMAN. LET'S OPEN YOU UP AND *TAKE A LOOK!*
RUUMMMMMBLE

RUUMMMMMBLE
FWOOOSSSHH
AH, MY FAITHFUL ETRIGAN. WOULD YOU REALLY HARM MY SERVANT?
BLAZE!

I HAD TURNED AWAY FROM YOU, MY LOVE, BUT I SEE YOU ONCE MORE.
EVEN WITHOUT YOUR RANK OF OFFICE, YOU ARE POWERFUL. RETURN TO ME AT ONCE, LOYAL ONE, AND I WILL GIVE YOU BACK YOUR RHYME.
POWER AND STATUS IN HELL. YOUR RIGHTFUL RANK RETURNED. COME TO ME AND TAKE IT BACK, MY LOVE.
YES... ANYTHING FOR THAT.
NOOO!
I AM IN CONTROL NOW, JASON BLOOD! I WILL HAVE MY POWER RETURNED!
I AM YOURS, DARK LADY.
THEN RISE.

NOW NOTHING CAN STAND IN OUR WAY.
IT IS TIME...

"...OUR ENEMIES STAND WAITING."
THANK YOU FOR BRINGING ME HERE FIRST, BUT I'M READY TO GO.
THIS PLACE BELONGS TO SOMEONE ELSE. I FEEL LIKE I WAS A DIFFERENT PERSON WHEN I WAS HERE LAST. LIKE I LIVED UNDER A FOG.
YOUR AMULET. I HAD IT FOR A VERY SHORT TIME, AND I ALMOST LOST MYSELF.
YOU HAD IT YOUR WHOLE LIFE.
AND NOW I'M FREE OF IT, BUT NOT OF HIM. MY FATHER IS STILL OUT THERE HUNTING ME.
"AFTER I LEFT MY FATHER FOR DEAD, I SPENT YEARS TRYING TO FIND MYSELF.
"I DIDN'T KNOW WHO I WAS, AND I FELT MORE COMFORTABLE SURROUNDED BY PARTIES AND DISTRACTIONS.
The Cat's Meow
"A FEW WEEKS AGO, I WAS LEAVING A NIGHTCLUB AFTER A LOT OF DRINKING AND DANCING.
"I TOLD THE DRIVER TO TAKE ME HOME.
"BUT WHEN HE TURNED, IT WAS SOME HORRIBLE MONSTER, INSTEAD. MY DRIVER WAS DEAD BESIDE IT.
"IT TOLD ME THAT I HAD DESERTED IT, BUT AFTER YEARS OF GROWING STRONGER, IT WAS READY TO RECLAIM ME AND TAKE MY SOUL."

"I PANICKED AS WE DROVE AWAY.
"I DON'T KNOW WHAT CAME OVER ME, BUT I WAS TERRIFIED. I JUST COULDN'T GO BACK THERE... THE MONSTER'S HEAD HIT THE WHEEL.
S
LITTLE JERRY'S
SARAH'S
"IT WAS MY FATHER. I KNEW IT. I DON'T KNOW HOW HE DID IT, BUT HE BEAT DEATH TO COME FOR ME!"
I JUST RAN, AND WHEN I WAS TAKEN BY CROC, I LET IT HAPPEN. ANYTHING WAS BETTER THAN BEING FOUND BY MY FATHER.
YOU CAN'T RUN FOREVER, DAWN.

WE'LL FACE THIS TOGETHER... ONCE AND FOR ALL.

BATMAN: THE DARK KNIGHT #5 cover
Art by **DAVID FINCH, SCOTT WILLIAMS** and **ALEX SINCLAIR**

Gotham City in the rain. Always makes me think of my parents.
It's like a steady pounding against your heart. It's the moment you lost all the things you can never have back.
Makes you cherish the golden dawn.

I keep asking myself, "Why?" Why risk everything for a girl I once knew?
But I already know the answer: Deep down, I'll do everything in my power to save her.

Because we were children together when my mother and father were still alive.
She's one of the few remaining things that connects me to them.

BATMAN? WHAT IS IT?
WHAT'S WRONG?

OH, MY--

DAWN! GET BEHIND ME AND STAY CLOSE!
I CAN'T--
JUST DO IT!

DAWN! STAY WITH ME! I'VE GOT YOU--

NO! YOU SAID YOU'D PROTECT ME!

BATMAN!
YOU PROMISED!

"YOU **PROMISED!**"

I promised.
But a promise is really just a break in the rain.

Sun comes out for a moment.
Just long enough to make you **hope.**

DAWN?

Then it always starts **raining** again.

BATMAN!
YOU'VE PAINED THE HEART OF MY LADY BLAZE!
EHHF!
AND THIS PAINS ME, IN TURN!
BUT MY LADY GRANTS A RETURN OF MY POWER! AND SO I'LL PASS YOU THAT PAIN A THOUSANDFOLD, DARK KNIGHT!
BEGINNING WITH THE CRACK OF YOUR HEAD!

IN THE SEWERS OF GOTHAM...
EX MALUM ABBAS ADVEHO MALUM FILIA! PROGNATUS IN INFECTUS VISCUS. PARVULUS QUISNAM MOS PRESTO MALUM FATUM! IS ADDO VITA ETERNUS!
EX MALUM BAS ADVEHO MALUM VISCUS. PARVULUS M MOS PRESTO FATUM! IS ADDO VITA ETERNUS!
EX MALUM VEHO MALUM OGNATUS IN CUS. PARVULUS MOS PRESTO FATUM! IS ADDO VITA ETERNUS!
EX MALUM BAS ADVEHO MALUM PROGNATUS IN VISCUS. PARVULUS M MOS PRESTO FATUM! IS ADDO A ETERNUS!
EX MALUM ABBAS ADVEHO MALUM FILIA! PROGNATUS IN INFECTUS VISCUS. PARVULUS QUISNAM MOS PRESTO MALUM FATUM! IS ADDO VITA ETERNUS!
ENOUGH!
EX MALUM ABBAS ADVEHO MALUM FILIA! PROGNATUS IN INFECTUS VISCUS. PARVULUS QUISNAM MOS PRESTO MALUM FATUM! IS ADDO VITA ETERNUS!
FROM THE UNHOLY FATHER COMES THE UNHOLY DAUGHTER. BORN INTO CORRUPTED FLESH. A CHILD OF UNHOLY DESTINY.
BRINGER OF LIFE ETERNAL!

EX MALUM ABBAS ADVEHO MALUM FILIA! PROGNATUS IN INFECTUS VISCUS. PARVULUS QUISNAM MOS PRESTO MALUM FATUM! IS ADDO VITA ETERNUS!
NNNHH--
UNDER THE DARK LIGHT OF REPUGNANT DAY...IN THE NURTURING BOSOM OF THE FIRES OF DARKEST HELL...I CALL UPON THE POWERS OF THE DARKEST NIGHT TO GRANT ME THE BOON OF ETERNITY!
MINE IS THE POWER, THE RIGHT OF MIGHT AND THE RIGHT OF ORDINANCE OVER THIS FLESH.
FOR THIS FLESH EXISTS THAT I MAY PARTAKE OF IT.
I TAKE THIS HUMAN ESSENCE, WRAPPED IN SKIN AND BONES. AS IT COMES INTO THIS WORLD IN A GLORIOUS SHUDDER OF PAIN, SO MAY IT LEAVE!
NOW. DAUGHTER.
LOOK UPON MY TRUE FACE...

THIS IS HOW IT FEELS TO FALL INTO THE ABYSS, BATMAN! SUFFER AS I HAVE!
NOW YOU WILL DIE--AS MY LADY COMMANDS!
I'M NOT YOUR ENEMY, ETRIGAN! SHE IS!
NO! TO HER, MY ALLEGIANCE! SHE RETURNED THE POWER I HAD LOST!
I AM THE INSTRUMENT OF YOUR DEMISE!
POONT
FSSSS
NO.

TNNK
KOOM
ALL I SEE IS SOMEONE FAMILIAR *FALLING.* BUT YOU DON'T KNOW HOW TO STOP YOURSELF FROM HITTING THE GROUND.
AND YOU NEVER WILL UNLESS YOU LEARN TO THINK FOR YOURSELF.

INSOLENT WRETCH!

HHH... ALL OF THAT POWER SHE GAVE YOU, ETRIGAN... IT'S THE DAMNDEST THING...
...EHH... I KNEW YOU WAY BACK WHEN...
...IF YOU'RE AS POWERFUL AS YOU ONCE WERE, WHAT HAPPENED TO YOUR RHYME?

THIS BAT NO LONGER AMUSES ME, MY LOVE. A BLISTER ON ITS HEART.
OPEN ITS SKIN AND SHOW ME THE GLISTENING PIECES THAT MAKE IT WORK.

MY SERVANT.

YOU SAID YOU WOULD GIVE ME BACK MY RHYME.

YOU DARE?
YOU DARE QUESTION MY INTENT, YOU GROVELING LITTLE MAGGOT?

I GAVE YOU POWER!

AND THIS IS HOW YOU REPAY ME?
ARRGH!

HA! THAT'S RIGHT, LITTLE ETRIGAN! WHERE'S THE FIRE IN YOUR BELLY? WHERE'S THE FLAME IN YOUR HEART?

GONE. BECAUSE ALL OF YOUR POWER NOW BELONGS TO ME!
NNN-NNHH--

WHERE I COME FROM, LADY--
--WE MAKE OUR OWN POWER.

THIS CAN'T BE HAPPENING...
OH, BUT IT IS HAPPENING. ALWAYS WAS.
I USED THE RAGMAN'S BODY AS A CONDUIT TO THIS WORLD, BUT I NO LONGER HAVE USE FOR HIM.
HELLO, MY LITTLE ONE.
DID YOU MISS DADDY?

I HAVE BEEN WITH YOU ALWAYS, DEAREST. YOU WERE EVER MY FLESH.
I RAISED YOU.
ALL FOR THIS ONE EXQUISITE MOMENT.
THAT YOU MAY IN TURN RAISE ME.

BACK AGAIN, AND HOW I'VE GROWN!
BUT THIS TIME I AM NOT ALONE!
BY MY SIDE YOU'LL FIND A NEW FOE!
CALL US THE DEMONIC DUO!

CRACKK
BATMAN!
BATMAN! OVER HERE-- PLEASE!
YOU'VE GOT TO S--
NO!
SHE WAS BORN IN UNHOLY FIRE, BATMAN! AND LIKE YOU, ALWAYS JUST A HAIR TOO LATE!
DID YOU REALLY THINK YOU COULD PREVENT THE BRAT FROM SERVING HER PURPOSE?

ETRIGAN! NOW!
BATMAN, THOUGH I SEE AND HEAR...
THERE ARE TOO MANY, I FEAR.
THERE ARE NEVER TOO MANY!
POOR LITTLE BAT...IS THAT ALL YOU CAME HERE TO SAY? TO TEACH AN OLD DOG A NEW TRICK?
TO MAKE ETRIGAN THINK HE COULD STAND AGAINST THE LIKES OF ME?
WELL, THEN, YOU THINK TOO...
...MUCH...
...NO... ETRIGAN...YOU DON'T HAVE THIS KIND OF POWER...

In my mind I see a big, beautiful kite. And it's floating away. And there's nothing I can do about it.
There's nothing I can ever do.
They all get blown away by the wind. Washed away by the rain.
All the ones I ever care for.
THE SPIRIT IS GONE, YOU MUST LET HER GO.
KNOW THAT YOU SAVED HER, EVEN SO.
A big, beautiful kite. And it's floating away. And there's nothing I can ever do.
But let it go.

EPILOGUE.
"DID YOU BRING THE SPECIFICATIONS OF THE BATMAN'S VEHICLE? CHOOSE YOUR WORDS CAREFULLY. YOUR FATHER'S LIFE DEPENDS UPON YOUR RESPONSE."
"I'M SORRY... I DID NOT."
"THEN TONIGHT YOUR FATHER WILL LOSE HIS HEAD..."
MI WILCOX
...AS HE BEGS FOR MERCY AT MY HAND, THINK ONLY THAT YOU COULD HAVE SAVED HIS LIFE, BUT INSTEAD, YOU BETRAYED HIM--
I HAVE SOMETHING BETTER INSTEAD, A DEVICE THAT FAR EXCEEDS YOUR EXPECTATIONS. AGAINST IT, THE BATMAN'S VEHICLE IS NOTHING.
WHAT IS IT?
A JAMMING DEVICE. WAYNE INDUSTRIES PERFECTED IT FOR THE BATMAN, HIMSELF. IT'S WHY EVEN THE FBI CAN NEVER TRACE HIS COMMUNICATIONS.
WHEN ACTIVATED IN THE VICINITY OF A SECURE COMPUTER, IT ALLOWS FREE COMMUNICATION WORLDWIDE, ENCRYPTED IN SUCH A WAY THAT NOT EVEN THE AMERICANS CAN BREAK THE CODES.
A WEAPON MAY KILL ONE MAN OR MANY. BUT THIS DEVICE GIVES YOU THE WORLD.
YOUR FATHER WILL BE SHOWN MERCY, GOD WILLING.
NOW GO.

DID THEY BELIEVE YOU?
YES.
AND THEY HAVE THE DEVICE MY SERVANT GAVE YOU?
YES.
THEN THEY'RE ABOUT TO GET *ME.*
THE END...

BATMAN: THE DARK KNIGHT #1 variant cover
Art by **DAVID FINCH**

FINCH
2010

BATMAN: THE DARK KNIGHT #1 variant cover
Art by **ANDY CLARKE**

BATMAN: THE DARK KNIGHT #2 variant cover
Art by **ANDY CLARKE** and **TOMEU MOREY**

BATMAN: THE DARK KNIGHT #3 variant cover
Art by **ANDY CLARKE** and **TOMEU MOREY**

BATMAN: THE DARK KNIGHT #4 variant cover
Art by **DAVID FINCH**

BATMAN: THE DARK KNIGHT #5 variant cover
Art by **ANDY CLARKE** and **TOMEU MOREY**

BATMAN: THE RETURN #1 cover
Art by **DAVID FINCH, SCOTT WILLIAMS** and **PETER STEIGERWALD**

BATMAN: THE RETURN
PLANET GOTHAM

GRANT MORRISON
Writer

DAVID FINCH
Penciller

BATT and RYAN WINN
Inkers

PETER STEIGERWALD
Colorist

DAVE SHARPE
Letterer

Bats are common on the eastern seaboard of the United States of America, and those three that moon-minted night were no less conventional than the rest of their breed.
A little bigger, a little more aggressive tonight perhaps, but otherwise unremarkable.
As insignificant in the great, great scheme of things as any other thing could **conceivably** be in any truly great scheme.
This particular bat, on that particular night, was just a common creature at the end of his forty-year lifespan.

As was the way of life in general, he'd been aware more and more often of others like him who were younger, fiercer and more likely to insist on the enforcement of strict territorial boundaries.
As was also the way, that night was inevitable.
That night was when something bigger...
Faster.
Smarter.
Younger.
Hungrier.
Better came along.
But this old bat...
This old bastard bat was not yet ready to die.
Not there, not then.

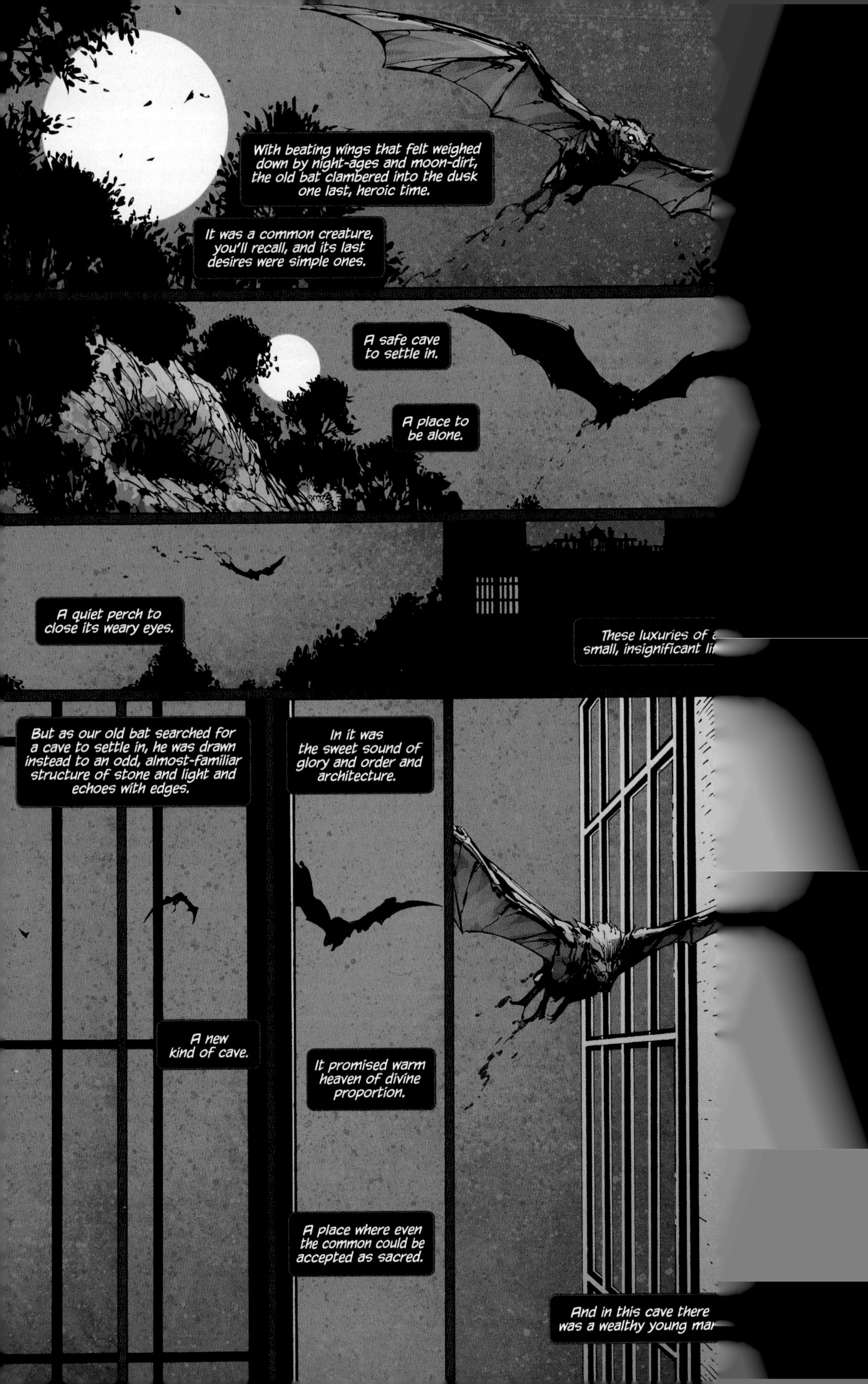

With beating wings that felt weighed down by night-ages and moon-dirt, the old bat clambered into the dusk one last, heroic time.
It was a common creature, you'll recall, and its last desires were simple ones.
A safe cave to settle in.
A place to be alone.
A quiet perch to close its weary eyes.
These luxuries of
small, insignificant
But as our old bat searched for a cave to settle in, he was drawn instead to an odd, almost-familiar structure of stone and light and echoes with edges.
In it was the sweet sound of glory and order and architecture.
A new kind of cave.
It promised warm heaven of divine proportion.
A place where even the common could be accepted as sacred.
And in this cave there
was a wealthy young

His name was Bruce Wayne and he was bleeding to death, hopeless, with a bell in his hand.
A lost knight without a standard.
A soldier with a wounded heart.
A warrior without a totem.
A life without meaning.

THAT'S IT.
And so was born this weird figure of the night!

YOU DIDN'T EXPECT TO SEE ME HERE, DID YOU?
THERE'S STILL TIME TO LET THE BOY GO, HUSSAIN MOHAMMED.
HOW DO YOU KNOW MY NAME?
I WON'T STOP NOW!
STAY BACK!
YOU DON'T KNOW LEVIATHAN.
YOU DON'T KNOW WHAT THEY DO TO PEOPLE.
I'D RATHER DIE!

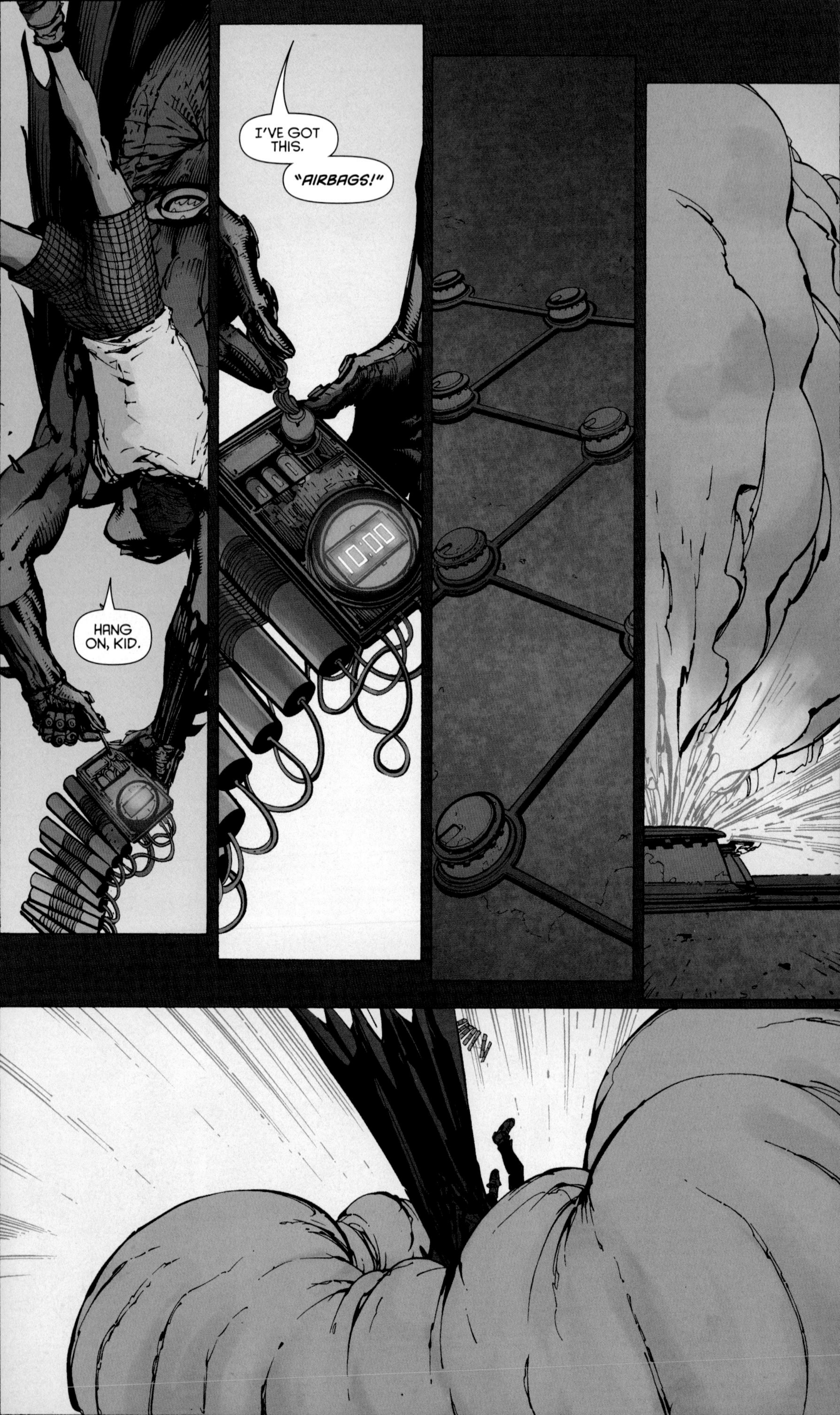
I'VE GOT THIS.
"AIRBAGS!"
HANG ON, KID.
10:00

HOW CAN I REWARD YOU?
THE BOY IS MY LIFE.
TAKE MONEY... CARS...
...J-JEWELS...
YOU HAVE NOTHING I WANT, FAROUK.
WHAT HUSSAIN KNOWS WILL DESTROY YOU.
AND I KNOW WHAT HUSSAIN KNOWS.
YOU'RE NEXT.
?

TWENTY-TWO HOURS LATER: THE BATCAVE.
WE TRUST
JOKER
JOKER

YOU ALL KNOW WHY I'VE ASKED YOU HERE.
AND IF YOU DON'T, PAY ATTENTION.
THIS IS THE BEGINNING OF SOMETHING NEW.

I WENT THROUGH A FEW FAIRLY UNUSUAL EXPERIENCES EVEN FOR *ME* RECENTLY.
YOU ALL KNOW I CONSIDER YOU MY *CLOSEST* CRIMEFIGHTING ASSOCIATES AND THAT'S WHY I'M *STARTING* THIS HERE, WITH ALL OF *YOU.*
WE'LL SPEAK INDIVIDUALLY. BUT YOU'LL EACH FIND SPECIAL *ASSIGNMENTS* IN THE ENVELOPES.
STARTING TODAY, WE FIGHT *IDEAS* WITH *BETTER IDEAS.*
THE IDEA OF *CRIME* WITH THE IDEA OF *BATMAN.*
FROM *TODAY* ON, BATMAN WILL BE EVERYWHERE IT'S *DARK,* NO PLACE TO *HIDE.*

YOUR RESPIRATION IS FASTER AND SHALLOWER.
YOU SEEM UNNATURALLY FOCUSED ON THIS WHOLE PRESENTATION.
ARE YOU SURE YOU'RE OKAY AFTER WHAT HAPPENED, BRUCE?
NEVER BETTER, BARBARA.
IN SPRING NEXT YEAR, WAYNETECH IS ANNOUNCING INTERNET 3.0.
I WANT YOU TO BE MY GHOST IN THE MACHINE.
YOU'LL HAVE ACCESS TO CHEAT CODES, VEHICLES AND WEAPONS NO ONE ELSE HAS.
OH, AND FEEL FREE TO CUSTOMIZE YOUR AVATAR-- DESIGN DIVISION...
INTERNET 3.0?
WHAT IS THIS?
WAIT A MINUTE.
YOU WANT ME TO ENROLL IN A FINISHING SCHOOL IN ENGLAND?
I HAVE A LIFE. I HAVE FRIENDS.
NEVER MIND THAT.
WHAT ABOUT US?
WHAT ABOUT BATMAN AND ROBIN?

TWO HOURS LATER: WAYNETECH R&D.
...I'M AUTHORIZING A MASSIVE CASH INJECTION, LUCIUS.
WE'RE INVESTING IN BLEEDING EDGE TECHNOLOGY AND WORKING PROTOTYPES TO SUPPORT BATMAN'S WAR ON CRIME.
TT
MY PLEASURE, MR. WAYNE.
THAT'S WHY WE'RE HERE.
IT'S GOOD TO HAVE YOU BACK TO YOUR OLD SELF.
THESE ARE THE LATEST TEST DRIVE MODELS.
MILITARY RECALL, CONSIDERED TOO RISKY FOR DEPLOYMENT, ALTHOUGH THE MODIFICATIONS I MADE TO THE KEYPAD SHOULD IRON OUT ANY BUGS.
IT MAY TAKE A LITTLE GETTING USED TO...
HH
THE G.I. ROBOT PROGRAM. RECALLED AFTER THEY RAN ROGUE.
I NEED A THOUSAND BY SPRING.
SOMETHING TOLD ME YOU'D SAY SOMETHING LIKE THAT.
IT OCCURRED TO ME THAT YOUR FRIEND BATMAN MIGHT BE VERY INTERESTED IN THE POTENTIAL OF REMOTE-CONTROLLED SOLDIERS.

I COULDN'T AGREE MORE.

WHAT *ELSE* HAVE YOU GOT FOR ME?

RIGHT THIS WAY, MISTER WAYNE.

...*JET-SUITS* INCREASE HUMAN STRENGTH AND ENDURANCE AS WELL AS PROVIDING *SHORT-RANGE FLIGHT* CAPABILITY.

AGAIN, CONSIDERED TOO *COSTLY* AND TOO RISKY FOR *OPERATIONAL* USE.

ALTHOUGH I CAN SEE *SEVERAL* WAYS TO *FIX* THAT...

INTERESTING.

HOW QUICKLY CAN YOU MODIFY *TWO* OF THESE?

A DAY?

TWELVE HOURS.

IN *BLACK*, I TAKE IT.

GO WILD.

WE WANT THEM TO LOOK LIKE *BATMAN AND ROBIN*, LUCIUS.

THIRTY HOURS LATER: YEMEN.

I'VE HEARD A LOT OF **GOOD THINGS.**

YOU LIKE WORKING WITH **DICK GRAYSON?**

HE'S ALL RIGHT.

WHY ARE **WE** HERE, FATHER?

AM I **ON TRIAL** IN SOME WAY?

HUSSAIN MOHAMMED CLAIMED HIS BROTHER HAD BEEN KIDNAPPED AND **OPERATED ON...**

...I DISCOVERED SHEIKH FAROUK WAS FINANCING ILLEGAL BIO-EXPERIMENTS **RIGHT HERE.**

DIRTY ENHANCEMENTS. METAGENE BOOSTERS, SYNTHETIC **SUPERPOWERS.**

WHAT ARE THEY?
SURGICALLY ENGINEERED SUPERHUMAN BODYGUARDS--ALL THE RAGE AMONG THE MEGA-WEALTHY. ASK YOUR MOTHER.
THESE LOOK LIKE FAILED EXPERIMENTS.
CANNON FODDER.
THE RUMOR IS THEY WERE WORKING ON A BIG SECRET PROJECT FOR A MYSTERY CLIENT.
AN ALPHA MODEL DESIGNER SUPERHUMAN.
STAY ALERT.
YOU HAVEN'T ANSWERED MY QUESTION.
WAS I RIGHT TO ASSUME THIS MISSION WAS SOME KIND OF TEST OF MY CONTINUED SUITABILITY AS ROBIN?
NOT AT ALL.
I'VE ALREADY MADE MY MIND UP ABOUT THAT.
...MY GOD...
THIS ONE'S STILL ALIVE BUT I THINK HER LARYNX HAS BEEN CRUSHED... I SEE FINGER MARKS...
ROBIN.
ARE YOU LISTENING?

VAMPIRE MAN!
TRAKTIR OF THE SUPER-COLLECTIVE IS HERE!
LEAVE HER BE OR DIE!
URHHH... IT STINKS DOWN THERE!
YOU SURELY DON'T NEED ME FOR THIS.
TARGETING LASERS.
STAY CLOSE BY THE WOMAN, HE WON'T SHOOT!
TRAKTIR IS LAST HERO STANDING!
I LOST MY COMPANIONS! MY WORLD IN FINAL CONFLICT WITH THE HERETIC!
I WILL NOT LOSE MY LAST LOVE!
MY SWEET SPIDRA!

DERANGED.
BLIND SPOT ON MY *LEFT.*
LET'S GET SOME *BLOOD* IN THOSE EYES...
HAAAURRR
ROBIN.
TAKE LEFT!
ROBIN, I SAID--
GUNNGF

ROBIN!
I'M NOT YOUR
ENEMY!
HERE IN FINAL ARENA ALL MEN ARE ENEMIES OF TRAKTIR!
GLAUUF
YOU'LL NEVER BREAK TRAKTIR!
TRAKTIR WILL NEVER FALL!
VAMPIRE MAN!
TRAKTIR, WAIT.
HER THROAT WAS CRUSHED BUT NOW SHE CAN BREATHE, SEE?
I SAVED HER LIFE. SPIDRA, RIGHT?
WHO DID THIS TO YOU BOTH?
SILO
THERE.
THAT CARCASS WAS HIS CRADLE.
THEY CALLED HIM "FATHERLESS"!

ROBIN!
I...I KNOW YOU...BUT...
...THAT DAY HAS YET TO COME.
WHEN IT DOES...

...YOU WILL KNOW ME.

STAY WHERE YOU ARE!
I AM CALLED.
GRAHH!
I MUST OBEY.
...WHAT ARE YOU?
YOU WILL KNOW ME.
BUT NOT--
YET!

TT

I GAVE ORDERS, ROBIN.
THIS IS NOT A GAME!

THAT'S IT!
I DIDN'T COME HERE TO BE PATRONIZED OR JUDGED ON MY "PERFORMANCE."
FIND ANOTHER ROBIN!
THE CHANCES OF OUR WORKING ON A REGULAR BASIS AS BATMAN AND ROBIN ARE ZERO, DAMIAN.
OW.
HARSH, BRUCE.
I NEED A PARTNER WHO CAN STAY FOCUSED AND KEEP UP.
BRUCE, COME ON! I MADE A CAREER OUT OF NOT DOING ANYTHING I WAS TOLD WHEN I WAS ROBIN.
HE GAVE UP EVERYTHING FOR THIS.
YOU CAN'T JUST TAKE IT AWAY.
WHAT MADE YOU THINK I'D DO THAT?
I'VE SEEN WHAT YOU'RE CAPABLE OF TOGETHER.
ALFRED, JIM GORDON... THEY LOVE YOU.
YEAH, WELL... YOU SHOULD SMILE MORE.
WHATEVER'S GOING ON BEHIND ALL THIS...
...YOU CAN'T CUT HIM OUT.
WHY WOULD I?
I AM STILL HERE.
YOU CAN TALK DIRECTLY TO ME.
I WANT YOU BOTH TO STAY TOGETHER, AS BATMAN AND ROBIN, HERE IN GOTHAM CITY.
LIKE YOU SAID, DAMIAN, "WE NEED ALL THE BATMEN WE CAN GET."
"BATMAN, INCORPORATED."
BRUCE, LOOK, I DID WHAT I COULD TO FILL IN, BUT THERE'S ONLY ONE BATMAN AND WE KNOW IT...
NO... NOT THIS TIME.
THIS TIME IT'S BIGGER THAN THAT.
I NEED YOU... GOTHAM NEEDS YOU.
THE WORLD NEEDS US.
OKAY.
THIS IS... BRUCE... WOW.
WHAT DO YOU SAY, ROBIN?
YOU MADE THE RIGHT DECISION, FATHER.
NOW.
PERHAPS NOW YOU'LL WANT TO KNOW ABOUT THE BUG I MANAGED TO PLANT WHEN I "DISOBEYED ORDERS."

...I CAN'T BELIEVE HOW MUCH THE BOY'S CHANGED...
SHE CAN'T BE HAPPY.
NEVERTHELESS, GOTHAM CITY IS IN VERY CAPABLE HANDS, SIR.
ALTHOUGH...
THERE'S A LOT YOU'VE NOT TOLD THEM YET, ISN'T THERE?
I HAVE TO PROTECT THEM FROM WHAT'S COMING... WHAT I SAW...
TOKYO. HOW DOES TOKYO SOUND FIRST, ALFRED?
THEN MAYBE ARGENTINA.
WE HAVE PROPERTIES ALL AROUND THE WORLD, MASTER BRUCE.
YOU RARELY VISIT THEM, BUT THEY ARE REGULARLY MAINTAINED.
I--
GOOD.
WE NEED MORE BATCAVES.
I'LL SEE TO IT RIGHT AWAY, SIR.
AND I'LL KEEP AN EYE ON THINGS THIS END, DON'T YOU WORRY ABOUT THAT.
THOSE YOUNG MEN WON'T LET YOU DOWN.
I KNOW... BUT THEY'RE ONLY THE START OF AN ARMY AGAINST CRIME...
IT FEELS GOOD TO BE BACK, OLD FRIEND.
AT THE BEGINNING OF SOMETHING AND NOT THE END.
INDEED.
WE SOLDIER ON UNDAUNTED, YOU AND I, MASTER BRUCE.
AND IF I MAY SAY SO, SIR...
...I COULDN'T BEG, BORROW OR STEAL A FINER WAY TO LIVE MY LIFE.

SELINA!
I JUST GOT BACK FROM THE DEAD AND THOUGHT OF YOU.
I NEED TO STEAL A SUPERWEAPON FROM THE LAIR OF A CRIMINAL MASTERMIND...
...YOU BUSY?
ALFRED.
TODAY IS A GOOD DAY.
HERE'S TO MANY MORE, SIR.

EIGHT HOURS LATER: LEVIATHAN.
...OUR FACILITY IN YEMEN WAS COMPROMISED, SHEIKH IBN ALI FAROUK.
IT IS, IN FACT, IN THE HANDS OF THE ENEMY.
NOR IS THAT THE MOST DISGRACEFUL MISTAKE YOU'VE MADE.
YOU ALMOST BROUGHT HIM HERE.
THE DARK KNIGHT.
HERE.
FORGIVE ME...I...
YOU KNOW I CAN'T HAVE THAT.
HE'LL LEARN NOTHING FROM ME, I ASSURE YOU.
I CAN ORGANIZE AN ARMY OVERNIGHT, RECAPTURE THE FACILITY...
...PLEASE...
BUT HOW DO WE TRULY AND EFFECTIVELY PUNISH A PROUD FATHER LIKE YOU?
THE MASTER DETECTIVE WILL KNOW OF US WHEN I DECIDE, NOT BEFORE.
AND IN THAT MOMENT, HE WILL DIE AT MY FEET.
YOU, MY DEAR SHEIKH, WILL NOT BE THERE, I FEAR, TO THANK THE BATMAN FOR SAVING YOUR SON'S LIFE...
FATHER.
I WAS SAVED TO PURIFY THE WORLD IN LEVIATHAN'S NAME.
IN THE NAME OF ALL THAT IS PURE AND TRUE, STRONG AND YOUNG, YOU CAN ONLY DIE.

MY SON... OMAR.
...PUT THE GUN DOWN...
MY DEAREST SON.
DIE.
HAIL LEVIATHAN.
AND SO WE WAIT, PATIENTLY.
OUR TENDRILS SPREADING, UNCHECKED, UNCONTROLLED, UNSEEN.
OUR HATRED VASTER THAN EMPIRES AND MORE SLOW. OUR NAME...
LEVIATHAN!
SKSKZZK
GAME ON.

ETERNAL

DAVID FINCH
Writer and Penciller

SCOTT WILLIAMS
Inker

PETER STEIGERWALD
Colorist

STEVE WANDS
Letterer

PLEASE CONNER, NOT TONIGHT.
I'M NOT HERE FOR A FIGHT, DAMIAN. JUST TO PAY MY RESPECTS. SAME AS YOU.
YES. A TRUCE. AT LEAST ON THIS DAY.

I WASN'T GOING TO COME THIS YEAR. I DON'T EVEN KNOW IF I BELIEVE ANYMORE.
DID YOU EVER? BELIEVE, I MEAN.
TRUCE, REMEMBER? I'M NOT UP FOR A FIGHT. EVEN IF IT'S JUST WORDS.
FINE.
TERRY IS DOING WELL. BUT HE'S UP AGAINST SUCH CHAOS OUT THERE. IT SCARES ME...THINKING ABOUT THE FUTURE.

I REMEMBER WHEN YOU WEREN'T AFRAID OF ANYTHING.
NO. THEN I WAS JUST AFRAID OF SHOWING WEAKNESS TO MY MOTHER AND FATHER. IT PUSHED ME TO THE EDGE. BUT FOR WHAT?
I WONDER IF I'M DOING RIGHT BY TERRY. IT'S SO MUCH TO PUT ON HIS SHOULDERS. I FOUGHT THE GOOD FIGHT MOST OF MY LIFE, AND I'M LEAVING HIM WITH A WORLD WORSE OFF THAN WHEN I STARTED.

DON'T YOU KNOW? DIDN'T BRUCE TEACH YOU ANYTHING AT ALL?

WE DO IT FOR THEM.
YOU HAVEN'T BEEN LISTENING! I'VE ALWAYS DONE IT FOR HIM! I NEVER WANTED TO LET HIM DOWN. BUT NOW HE'S GONE, AND I HAVE NOTHING!
NO, DAMIAN. YOU'RE LOOKING IN THE WRONG PLACE.
READ THE INSCRIPTION.
IN LOVING MEMORY OF THE WORLD'S FINEST HEROES ERECTED BY THE CHILDREN OF THOSE SAVED
WE DO IT FOR THEM. THE FAMILIES THAT EXIST BECAUSE WE WERE THERE. THE LIVES THAT WE TOUCH ARE OUR LEGACY. THAT'S WHY WE NEVER STOP FIGHTING.
THAT'S WHY SUPERMAN AND BATMAN CAN NEVER DIE.
END

FINCH
2010

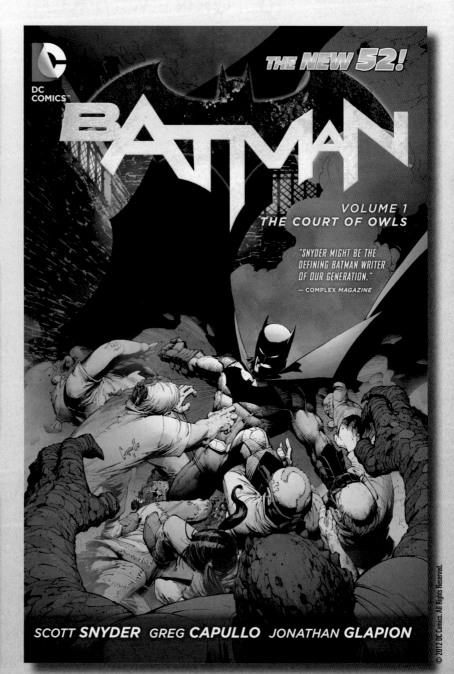

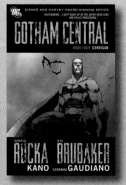

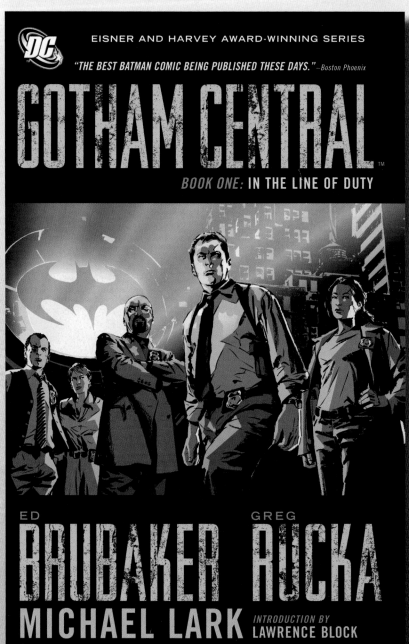

"Game-changing redefining of the Caped Crusader."
—ENTERTAINMENT WEEKLY SHELF LIFE

"A wildly entertaining ride that's been at all times challenging, unsettling, amusing, inventive, iconic and epic... one of the most exciting eras in Batman history."
—IGN

FROM *NEW YORK TIMES* #1 BEST-SELLING WRITER

GRANT MORRISON

with ANDY KUBERT

BATMAN: THE BLACK GLOVE

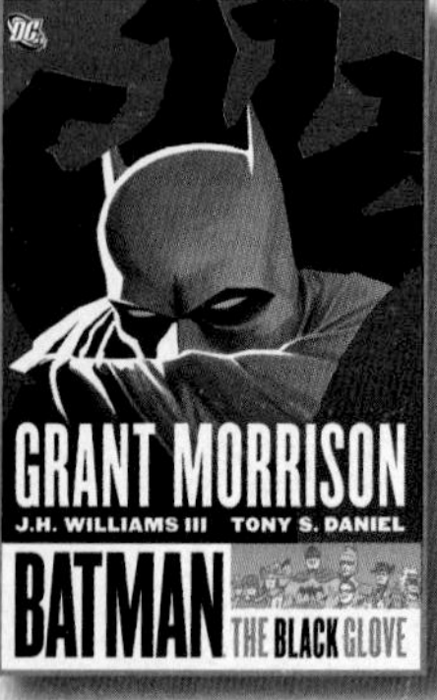

with J.H. WILLIAMS III and TONY S. DANIEL

BATMAN: R.I.P.

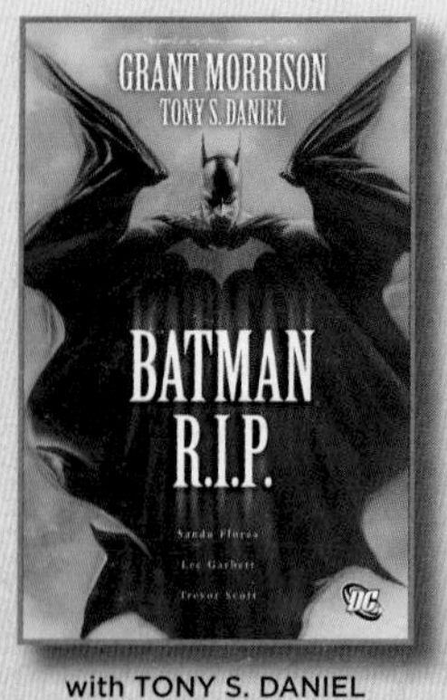

with TONY S. DANIEL

BATMAN: THE RETURN OF BRUCE WAYNE

with FRAZER IRVING, RYAN SOOK and other top talent